A Hiking Guide to
the Trails of Florida

A Hiking Guide to the Trails of Florida

Elizabeth F. Carter

Menasha Ridge Press
Birmingham, Alabama

Library of Congress Cataloging-in-Publication Data
Carter, Elizabeth F., 1939–
  A hiking guide to the trails of Florida.

  Bibliography: p.
  Includes index.
    1. Hiking—Florida—Guide-books. 2. Trails—Florida—
Guide-books. 3. Florida—Description and travel—
1981– —Guide-books. I. Title.
GV199.42.F6C37 1987   917.59   87-24724
ISBN 0-89732-068-9

Menasha Ridge Press
3169 Cahaba Heights Road
Birmingham, AL 35243

This book is dedicated to Butch Horn, a great chauffeur, photographer, and environmentalist, who is also my husband.

Contents

Acknowledgments

It was Winston Churchill who said that "writing a book is an adventure; to begin with it is a toy and an amusement, then it becomes a master, and then it becomes a tyrant; and the last phase is just as you are about to be reconciled to your servitude—you kill the monster and fling him . . . to the public." Writing this book has been all of the things that Churchill described: an adventure, an amusement, a master, and a tyrant. It has also been a lot of fun! A large part of the fun was meeting the people around Florida who gave so generously of their time to give me the information and guidance that I needed to make this book accurate and informative for you, the reader.

My special thanks to the personnel at the Florida Department of Natural Resources: Dr. Elton Gissendanner, Ney Landrum, Ellison Hardee, and Pete Hartsfield who made it possible for me to go to so many places and see a lot of things in a limited amount of time. Other DNR folks who were of assistance were Ken Alvarez, Charles Brannaka, Roger Cuenot, Jim Dixon, Phil Gearhart, Sam Graf, Al Green, Paul Perras, Phillip Rand, Dave Randall, Benny Woodham, and my husband, Butch Horn. At the Florida Department of Agriculture, Division of Forestry, my thanks to Phil Chessman; at Everglades National Park, Dick Martin; at St. Marks Refuge, Robin Wills; and, at the Florida State Library, Beverly Byrd and Barbara Mallock.

Very special thanks go to Mary Ann Twyford who works for DNR but is also my source of information on the Florida Trail Association, to author Betty Watts who is an inspiration to us all, and to my dear friends Dick and Barbara Gearhart who are not only good sports but are also photogenic.

Introduction

Welcome to hiking in Florida. When you take that first step, you will become one of a distinguished group who have chosen to see one of the most beautiful areas in the world from up close—on foot. That group includes Ponce de León, Hernando de Soto, William Bartram, Andrew Jackson, the "Barefoot Mailman," John Muir, Senator "Walkin' Lawton" Chiles, and many others. You are indeed fortunate that in many cases you can still see what they saw: a rich and variable land, well preserved and carefully maintained in its natural state.

Florida's landscape varies from Appalachian foothills, to coastal lowlands, to snow white beaches, to sweeping prairies. The variety of plants, animals, terrain, and waterways is unequalled by any other state, and there are more species of trees growing in Florida than anywhere else in the United States. Florida alone has more springs than any country in the world—over 300 of them. The vast array of flowers ranges from those common to the mountains to the exotic blooms of the tropics. The species of birds seen in Florida number in the thousands and animals and reptiles of all types and sizes are still roaming free in vast areas of undeveloped country. You cannot enjoy these wonders from an automobile. It is possible to ride by the same spot hundreds of times and never know that a rare plant grows there, that an endangered crocodile is swimming a few feet away, or that a crystal-clear spring is hidden under an ordinary limerock outcrop. To know Florida you must make a closer acquaintance.

For many years visitors to Florida have been perceived as passersby on their way to the hotels and beaches of the coasts, or as families en route to Disney World or other attractions. These are the goals of many of our guests, but there is an increasing interest in the other recreational resources that Florida has to offer. From the ridges and "steepheads" of northern Florida to the sawgrass prairies of the Everglades, each area of Florida has its own special character, its own unique personality. Don't assume that what can be seen from a car is all there is to see or you will deny yourself an opportunity to know the real Florida, the natural Florida.

1

Bear Gap Road Trail, Tosohatchee State Reserve

Despite a reputation for heat, humidity, and bugs, getting out-of-doors in Florida can be a pleasant and rewarding experience. Over half of the state is not semitropical and enjoys a change of seasons. It is said that spring in the continental United States begins in northern Florida, and the fall season is crisp and beautiful with impressive displays of colorful leaves. Winters are mild with just enough cool weather to put a snap in the air. In the southern section, sunny winter days provide a wonderful opportunity to get out and explore, and spring and fall are incredibly lovely.

A state that is still over 12 percent "wilderness," Florida is blessed with state and local leaders who are aware of the need to conserve and preserve its natural resources. Over 8 million acres of the state are in public ownership: 4.25 million acres of federal lands and 4.7 acres of state lands. And the acquisition of ecologically significant and endangered areas continues. At the time of this writing, the U.S. Congress is considering a huge addition to the Big Cypress National Preserve, the State of Florida is purchasing more of Fakahatchee Strand, and a recent purchase in the Big Bend added 64,000 acres to the public domain. Public ownership insures that these areas will be protected and maintained and that you will have access to them.

Natural History

The state of Florida is a landmass occupying a minor portion of the Floridian Plateau. This plateau, attached to the continental United States, is a partially submerged platform about 500 miles long and varies from 250 to 400 miles wide. It has existed for millions of years and is one of the most stable places on the earth's crust.

Over the millennia, Florida has been submerged under and resurfaced from a series of ancient seas. The Coastal Lowlands are the most recent landmasses to have emerged from the sea. They include areas that surround the hills in the Highlands of the northern and western sections of the state and they make up the flatlands that are known as south Florida.

The Highlands of north and west Florida are geologically much older than the Coastal Lowlands and they reach their highest point at about 325 feet above sea level. The ridges of the Panhandle are the last remains of the Appalachian Mountains. Proceeding southward, there are many terraces and ledges that were left on the landscape with the recession of the ancient seas. Along the more than 1,200 miles of coastline there are sandy beaches, saltwater marshes, saltwater swamps, and even rocky shoreline.

The most commonly encountered plant community in Florida is longleaf-slash pine forest or pine flatwoods. These are usually large tracts of high, well-drained, fairly level land dominated by pines. Hardwood hammocks are groups of hardwood trees and shrubs that are usually clustered around creeks, streams, or wet spots in the pine forests. Swamp forests are more densely wooded areas that may contain cypress and large hardwoods; they often border rivers and streams. Cypress swamps are also found along riverbanks but may occur as "strands" in low wet areas. Dry prairies are wide plains lacking trees, like those in the Lake Okeechobee area, while wet prairies are freshwater marshes. Salt marshes are found near beaches and bays as are mangrove swamps. Beaches are the shores of the ocean, the gulf, or of bays.

Along the southern rim of the state, mangrove swamp, swamp forest, and coastal saltwater marsh are most often encountered. The

3

Everglades primarily consist of freshwater marsh with wet and dry prairies, but pine flatwoods and hardwood hammocks are also seen there. In central Florida, pine flatwoods predominate, with mixed oak and hardwood hammocks and some cypress swamps present also. The Panhandle is largely pine flatwoods with some cypress swamp.

The types of plant, bird, and animal life that you will encounter along the trail are influenced by the type of plant communities that are present, which in turn are a result of the types of soils, underlying geologic conditions, and weather cycles that occur there.

Yearling deer on trail, Prairie Lakes State Preserve

Doug Sphar

Friendly Advice

Without going into great detail, we would like to share with you some information based on our experiences hiking and camping in Florida.

Insects

During the warm months mosquitoes, sandgnats, and yellow flies can be a source of great discomfort. Mosquitoes are usually confined to shady, wooded areas and are at their worst just at dusk and in the early morning, but in the Everglades and coastal swamps they may be active all day. Most commercial insect repellents are effective in discouraging them, but sweat may wash it off your skin leaving you vulnerable. Take lots of repellent to be sure that you are covered for the duration of your outing. Yellow flies are usually present on hot, still days and are rarely a problem after dark. They too are repelled by most commercial products, but it takes lots and every piece of exposed skin must be covered. Sandgnats, or no-see-ums, are the reason that good tents have fine netting on the doors and windows. Sandgnats are most common in marshy areas near the coast but will occasionally be encountered inland. Insect repellent alone does not deter them, but application of something oily to the skin will help. Some cosmetic bath oils, or baby oil mixed with repellent, are useful for this purpose.

Reptiles

There are several varieties of poisonous snakes in Florida, but the chances that you will see one are slight. Of the last 85 million visitors to Florida, only five were bitten by poisonous snakes and no one died. Use common sense when walking in the woods; never climb on or step over logs without checking for snakes and avoid walking in palmetto palms or into dense underbrush.

Alligators are another matter. There aren't more alligators than snakes, they are just easier to see! The Florida Game and Fresh Water

Fish Commission estimates that there are at least one million alligators in Florida but admits that there could be as many as two million. If you hike in an area that includes ponds, lakes, swamp, or coastal estuaries, your chances of seeing an alligator are very good. Avoid approaching or annoying them in any way. In some more populated areas where alligators have become accustomed to people, they are no longer shy and may be extremely dangerous.

Camping

Most of the longer trails in this book have designated camping areas. In situations where they do not, but camping is allowed, choose clearings on high ground. Camping in the swamp can be risky and uncomfortable. If possible, avoid camping near roadways or in areas that show evidence of heavy use by local folk. A quiet clearing beside a dirt road may turn into a local party spot after dark.

Property Rights

The trails described in this book are located on public property; but if you are confronted by a landowner, don't argue, just move on. Some public areas still have privately owned outholdings, or this book may be wrong! It goes without saying that No Trespassing and Posted signs should always be obeyed.

Leaving Cars Unattended

Some guidebooks will make suggestions about where you may safely leave cars. We prefer to let you use your own judgment. It is always best to arrange with someone to look after your car, and a small fee is worth the peace of mind.

Weather

While the bugs can be repelled and the reptiles avoided, the weather must be confronted. Northern Florida's mean average temperature is 68 degrees, with mild days occurring from October through December, followed by periods of very chilly weather until late February. March through June is usually very pleasant. During the humid months of July, August, and September afternoon thundershowers are a common occurrence.

Southern Florida's weather is temperate the year round; the mean average temperature there is 70 degrees. There may be an occasional cool spell in January or February, and the summer months are muggy and hot. Again, it rains more in the summer—usually afternoon thundershowers.

Be alert to the danger of lightning! If you are hiking on a prairie or open area crouch on the ground or in a depression or ditch during the storm. Never shelter under a tree and avoid being the tallest object around. Before setting out on a hike of any duration check the local weather report and set out prepared.

What to Take with You

There are as many opinions about what is essential hiking gear as there are hikers. Use your judgment or the advice of an expert outfitter. Our essentials for any Florida walk out of sight of the car are insect repellent and a hat. For anything more than a stroll, add water, rain gear, and Band-Aids! For more than three or four miles, carry a snack as well. Of course, the farther you go, the more you will need, and overnight camping elevates you into an entirely different level of specialized equipment.

Butch Horn

Torreya Trail

How to Use This Book

This directory of hiking trails was written to assist you in getting to know natural Florida. All of the trails included are on publicly owned land except where specifically noted, and all have public access and egress. Some of the trails will be immediately accessible to you, i.e., you may go there and hike with no further information or preparation. Some have adequate directions and/or information at the trail head or at a nearby location. For others you will need to secure maps or information ahead of time, and some may even require advance reservations. Our goal is to inform you about where the trails are, what they are like, what you may expect to see, and how to go about hiking on them. This is not a mile-by-mile guidebook. Specific information of that type is available on some of the trails and can be obtained from the sources named at the end of each trail description.

Many of the trails described in this book are also part of the Florida National Scenic Trail (or The Florida Trail). The Florida Trail Association has cleared and maintains this extensive trail system, much of which is on private property and is open only to members of the Association. Only those sections of The Florida Trail that are on public property are included here. Hikers who are interested in those trails should become members of the FTA and obtain a copy of their guidebook, *Walking the Florida Trail*, by John M. Keller. For more information, write to Florida Trail Association, P.O. Box 13708, Gainesville, FL 32604.

The National Trails System Act provides for three types of trails: National Scenic Trails, such as The Florida Trail, National Recreation Trails, and Connecting and Side Trails. Recreation Trails by law must be "reasonably accessible to urban areas or be located in state or national parks and forests," and Connecting and Side Trails "provide additional points of public access to nationally designated trails." Some of the trails in this directory are National Recreation Trails and this fact will be noted when appropriate.

A "trail" is defined as a path or track, and a "hike" is a march or tramp. Nowhere are we told how long the path must be to constitute a trail or how far we must march or tramp to have been on a hike! Therefore, for purposes of this directory, a hiking trail will be a path at least three miles long. Shorter trails are usually thought of as "nature walks." Although space will not permit an extensive review of these mini-trails, they should not be ignored. There are dozens of them throughout Florida and they provide a very beautiful and informative resource for outdoor recreation. One of the best ways to learn about the characteristics of an area is to go to the nearest state park or public recreation facility and walk the nature trail.

The Trails

For organizational purposes, the trails in this book have been divided into five sections: Trails of Northwest Florida, Coastal Trails of Northwest Florida, Trails of North and Northeast Florida, Trails of Central Florida, and Trails of South Florida.

Trails of Northwest Florida begin in the western Panhandle and proceed easterly to the Apalachicola National Forest near Tallahassee. The Coastal Trails of Northwest Florida begin at the St. Joseph Peninsula and go easterly along the coast, taking in the barrier islands of St. George and St. Vincent, and the St. Marks National Wildlife Refuge.

The North and Northeast Florida Trails begin on the east side of the Suwannee River at Manatee Springs and go northerly to O'Leno State Park, Osceola National Forest, Cary State Forest, and Ft. Clinch State Park at the Georgia line. They then proceed southerly along the coast to Little Talbot Island, inland to Gold Head Branch, Rice Creek, Bulow Creek, and to the Ocala National Forest.

The Central Florida Trails begin at the Withlacoochee State Forest and go easterly to Wekiwa Springs and Tosohatchee near Orlando. Then they follow the coast to Canaveral National Seashore and Merritt Island National Wildlife Refuge. From the coast, they go inland to the Prairie Lakes, Kissimmee Lakes, and Lake Arbuckle trails.

The South Florida Trails begin on the coast at Jonathan Dickinson State Park, go south to Loxahatchee National Wildlife Refuge and Biscayne National Park. They then go south and west through the Everglades National Park, Big Cypress Preserve, the Fakahatchee Strand, and Collier-Seminole State Park. They circle the tip of Florida and go north to Sanibel Island and then to Myakka River State Park near Sarasota.

Information regarding access, trail ending, camping, and difficulty follows each description. In order to condense this information into a small space, the following abbreviations were used: CR for county road, SR for state road, NFR for national forest road, and SFR for state forest road. Access is always given as a point found on the official Florida Transportation Map. Every effort has been made to keep directions on paved and well-marked roads. The reader should bear in mind that roads change and conditions alter. It is always wise to utilize local resources such as rangers and park managers to get up-to-date information and advice.

At the end of the book, a listing of "Other Trails" gives resources for hiking that are primarily in urban areas or that came to my attention too late for actual exploration.

Doug Sphar

Cypress on a sandbar seen from the trail along the Suwannee River

Trails of Northwest Florida

The Jackson Red Ground Trail
Blackwater River State Forest
21.5 miles

Sweetwater Trail
Blackwater River State Forest
4.5 miles

Pine Log Trail
Pine Log State Forest
3.0 miles

Torreya Trail
Torreya State Park
7.0 miles

Apalachicola Trail
Apalachicola National Forest
22.0 miles

Camel Lake Trail
Apalachicola National Forest
4.0 miles

The Jackson Red Ground Trail

Blackwater River State Forest
Okaloosa, Santa Rosa counties (near Milton)
21.5 miles

The Jackson Red Ground Trail is part of the National Recreational Trail System and is also a part of The Florida Trail. It was an Indian trading path that was used by General Andrew Jackson on his second trip to Florida in 1818. In early May of that year, General Jackson left Ft. Gadsden on the Apalachicola River with 1,200 men and traveled 225 miles to Pensacola in 18 days. General Jackson probably rode a horse most of the way, but his followers certainly earned a place as early Florida hikers. The name "red ground trail" is a result of the bright orange and red colors found in much of the soil of the area.

The trail is completely within the boundaries of the Blackwater River State Forest and frequently crosses and/or follows roads that are maintained by the State Forestry Department. It passes through fine examples of northern Florida pine flatwoods with occasional hammocks of swamp forest. The predominant trees are longleaf pines. They are found in the highlands accompanied by turkey, laurel, and live oaks, with an undercover of wiregrass. Slash and loblolly pines can be seen in the damper areas along with maple, sweetgum, blackgum, and other hardwoods. In the swamp forests, various oaks, sweetbay, magnolia, and cypress trees will be seen. Along the banks of the streams, the Atlantic white cedar shares space with bald cypress and spruce pines. The wide variety of trees, especially hardwoods, provides beautiful color in the fall, while in the spring, wild azalea—with pink, white, and yellow blooms—and the white-blooming titi make a splendid floral display.

The forest supports a diversity of small animals, including deer, fox, rabbits, squirrels, skunks, opossums and raccoons, but the hiker is much more likely to encounter bird life. Turkey and bobwhite quail are frequently seen and the longleaf pine stands are excellent habitat for the red-cockaded woodpecker.

Trees, flowers, animals, and birds notwithstanding, this area's most outstanding characteristic is its remarkable blackwater streams. Stained by tannins to the color of weak tea, these shallow, swift streams are noted for their clarity and for their huge white sandbars. The trail begins on beautiful Juniper Creek and crosses the Blackwater River. Hikers will welcome the opportunity to take a cool dip or at least a refreshing break beside one of these lovely waterways.

Begin: At Red Rock Picnic Area, 12 miles northeast of Milton, off CR 191.

End: At Karick Lake Recreation Area off CR 189.

Other Access: Mile 7 (SR 4), mile 9.6 (SFR 47), mile 17.7 (SFR 57).

Camping: At Red Rock (no facilities). Shelters and hand water pumps at mile 6.1 and at mile 12. Karick Lake has tables, pit toilets, and potable water.

Difficulty: Easy.

For Further Information: Blackwater River State Forest Headquarters, Rt. 1, Box 77, Milton, FL 32570. The Forest Headquarters is located at Munson, on SR 4, about 25 miles northeast of Milton. (904) 957-4201

Sweetwater Trail

Blackwater River State Forest
Okaloosa County (near Milton)
4.5 miles

This side trail to the Jackson Red Ground Trail was named after nearby Sweetwater Creek. It is similar to the main trail in terrain and characteristics and makes a pleasant short hike.

Begin: On the north side of SR 4.

End: At Krul Recreation Area.

Camping: Bear Lake Recreation Area at mile 3.0 has camping facilities and water. Krul Lake has an improved camping area with showers and other amenities. (Note: Camping in the vicinity is available at the Blackwater River State Park and at Hurricane Lake Recreation Area. Full facilities are available at these locations.)

Difficulty: Easy.

For Further Information: See above.

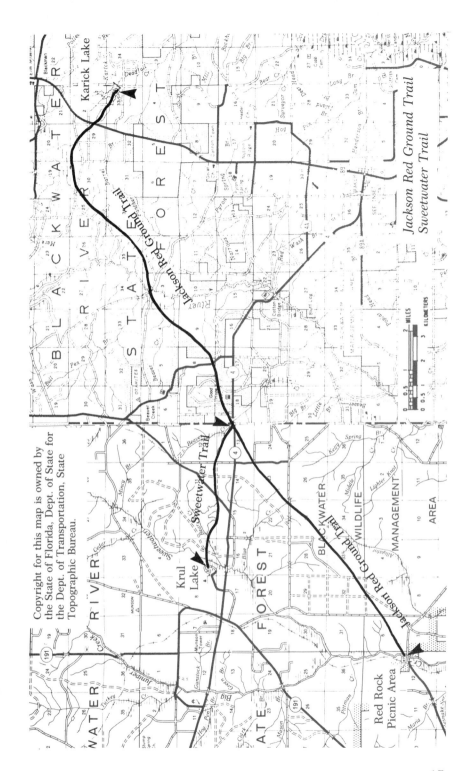

Jackson Red Ground Trail
Sweetwater Trail

15

Pine Log Trail

Pine Log State Forest
Bay County (near Ebro)
3.0 miles

In 1824, a Captain Burke was commissioned by the Florida Territorial Convention to build a road from Tallahassee to Pensacola. While surveying for this east to west route, he encountered a party of "citizen laborers" laying out a north to south road from Choctawhatchee "Big Spring" to St. Andrews Bay. This early road probably passed near or through what is now the Pine Log State Forest. It must have been a beautiful route in territorial days, bordering the swamps of the Choctawhatchee River and bypassing myriad sparkling "sandhill" ponds and lakes. When the state bought the property in 1935, it had been severely cut over and scarred by annual fires. Soon it was planted in slash, sand, longleaf, and loblolly pine and it is now a mature forest once more.

The three-mile nature trail at Pine Log has been recently included in the Florida National Scenic Trail system. It begins near the ranger residence and, passing by a small lake, winds through upland pine forests and along the banks of Pine Log Creek. In addition to this designated trail, the forest has miles of improved forest roads that are suitable for hiking.

A variety of habitats are present in the forest with an accompanying diversity of bird life. Look for those species found in the Blackwater Forest, plus nests of prothonotary and hooded warblers.

Begin: At Pine Log State Forest Headquarters just off SR 79, one mile south of Ebro.

End: Same place; this is a loop trail.

Additional Information: There is a new 6.9 mile trail.

Camping: In the campground just north of the trail head; all facilities are provided and it is located on a very pretty lake.

Difficulty: Easy.

For Further Information: Pine Log State Forest, Fla. Division of Forestry, Chipola River District, 1715 W. 15th St., Panama City, FL 32401. (904) 872-4175

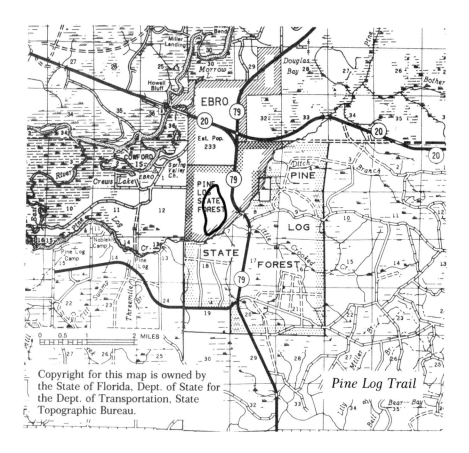

Pine Log Trail

Torreya Trail

Torreya State Park
Liberty County (near Bristol)
7.0 miles

The Torreya Trail is probably the most unique trail in Florida. In character it is much more similar to areas in the Appalachian Mountains than to a coastal region. Historically, according to whom you believe, it was first populated by either Adam and Eve or by early native Indian tribes. A Bristol attorney, E. E. Calloway, believed that there was evidence to support this site as the original "Garden of Eden," and he wrote a book promoting that idea. More scientific minds prefer the visible evidence of Indian mounds to confirm their theories. Territorial records indicate that Andrew Jackson crossed the Apalachicola River at this site in 1818 on his jaunt from Ft. Gadsden to Pensacola.

The most striking aspect of the trail is the contrast between high bluffs overlooking the Apalachicola River and the deep ravines that stretch behind the bluffs. Hundreds of plants common to the Appalachian Mountains are found in the area and include mountain laurel, wild ginger, and wild hydrangea. Plant communities include river swamp, hardwood hammock, high pineland, and cypress-gum swamp. Wildlife such as deer, beaver, bobcat, and grey fox inhabit the area and over 100 species of birds call it home. In all, there are 111 rare and endangered species found in the state park. The Florida yew or Torreya—the tree for which the trail was named—is among the very rare species that can readily be seen along the trail.

Although this is not a long hike, there are two primitive camping areas available. The Creek primitive area is at mile 0.75 near the beginning of the trail, and the River primitive area is at mile 3. Camping areas are limited to 12 persons and campers must register with the ranger. There is also camping with all facilities at the campground at the State Park.

Begin: At Torreya State Park, located 13 miles northeast of Bristol off SR 12.

End: Same place; this is a loop trail.

Camping: On the trail or at Torreya State Park.

Difficulty: Moderate.

For Further Information: Torreya State Park, Rt. 2, Box 70, Bristol, FL 32321. (904) 643-2674

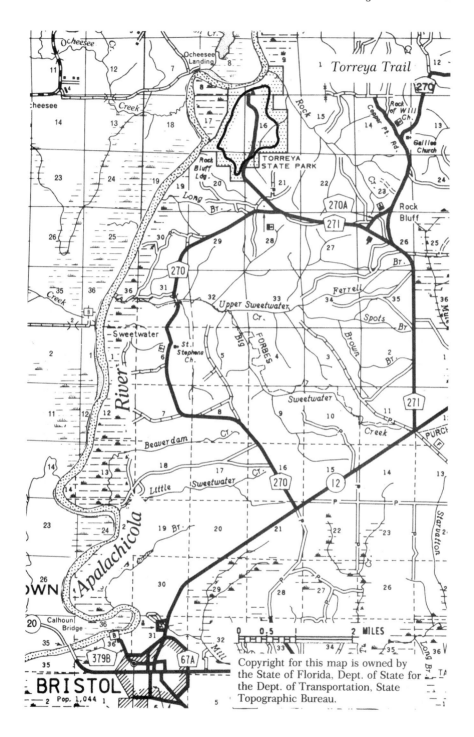

Apalachicola Trail

Apalachicola National Forest
Wakulla County (near Tallahassee)
22 miles

The Apalachicola National Forest is a vast (557,000-acre) preserve containing impressive examples of north Florida's many natural phenomena. There are four rivers that either border the forest or are enclosed by it—the Apalachicola, the Ochlockonee, the Sopchoppy, and the New; several smaller streams including Monkey, Lost, and Fisher creeks traverse it. It contains both Wilderness and Scenic Areas. Upland pine woods with sandy soil predominate, but there are some notable swamp areas, small lakes and ponds, sinkholes, swampy bays, hardwood hammocks, and beautiful corridors of cypress along the river banks.

The Apalachicola Trail crosses the Bradwell Bay Wilderness Area, one of the original wilderness areas established under the Wilderness East legislation. The area is home to a wide diversity of common as well as rare and endangered wildlife species. A "bay" of this type is a large, saucer-like depression in the terrain. The topography is flat and the water level is very close to the surface. This results in shallow water standing in many parts of the bay most of the year, except in very dry weather. Only experienced and properly equipped hikers should attempt this section of the trail.

Other sections of the trail follow the Sopchoppy River and Monkey Creek. These are lovely tea-colored streams with an abundance of hardwoods and other interesting vegetation. Birds to watch for include the red-cockaded woodpecker, which is most often seen in stands of mature long leaf pine. When hiking beside the streams, watch for swainsons's, hooded, and Kentucky warblers. Osprey may be sighted around lakes and ponds. Animals of the forest include such north Florida natives as raccoons, opossums, bear, and the American alligator. Some literature suggests that the Florida panther may still survive in this area, but it has been many, many years since one has been seen here.

The Apalachicola Trail is part of the Florida National Scenic Trail, is maintained by the Florida Trail Association, and is blazed with the FTA's characteristic orange blazes. It begins at Porter Lake Bridge on county road 368, but the first three miles are on private property and hikers must be members of the FTA to use it. Access on public property begins at forest road 314 (mile 4.9), but this is also the entrance to Bradwell Bay. Hikers who do not wish to traverse Bradwell Bay should enter the trail from forest road 329 (mile 12.8) and may continue to the terminus at US 319.

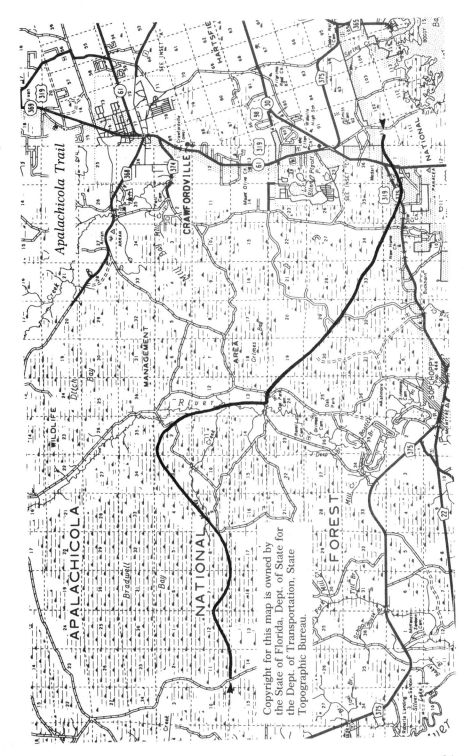

Copyright for this map is owned by the State of Florida, Dept. of State for the Dept. of Transportation, State Topographic Bureau.

21

Butch Horn

On the way to the Apalachicola Trail

There are no specifically designated campsites along the trail but camping is permitted. Water may be obtained from the rivers and streams, but must be treated before being used for drinking.

Begin: At NFR 314, about 23 miles south of the community of Bloxham, off CR 375. From Bloxham, travel south on CR 375 to the intersection with NFR 13. Turn left (east) on NFR 13 and continue for two miles to the junction with NFR 314. Turn right (south) on NFR 314 and continue for just over five miles to the FTA marker on the left.

End: On US 319, near the town of Sopchoppy. From Sopchoppy travel east on US 319 for 4.5 miles to the FTA marker on the left. This is less than two miles from the intersection of US 319 with US 98.

Note: Excellent maps of the Apalachicola National Forest are available from the District Ranger. It is essential to have these maps before setting out.

Camping: On the trail or in any of a number of designated campgrounds including Silver Lake, Mack Landing, Wood Lake, or at Ochlockonee River State Park.

Difficulty: Moderate to strenuous.

For Further Information: The District Ranger, Apalachicola National Forest, P.O. Box 309, Crawfordville, FL 32327. (904) 926-3561

Camel Lake Trail

Apalachicola National Forest
Liberty County (near Bristol)
4 miles

This trail is a four-mile loop in the western part of the forest, that leads from Camel Lake to Sheep Island Pond, and back. It traverses primarily upland pine woods and some hardwood hammocks and swamp areas. It is also part of the Florida National Scenic Trail and is blazed accordingly. Camping is permitted at Camel Lake, where potable water and some facilities can be found. Trails of this type provide hikers with a "sampler" of local terrain, flora, and fauna, without being strenuous or requiring a lot of preparation.

Begin: At Camel Lake Recreation Area, 15 miles south of Bristol off CR 379.

End: Same place; this is a loop trail.

Camping: At Camel Lake Recreation Area.

Difficulty: Easy.

For Further Information: The District Ranger, Apalachicola National Forest, P.O. Box 578, Bristol, FL 32321. (904) 643-2282

Carol Casey

Anhinga drying its wings

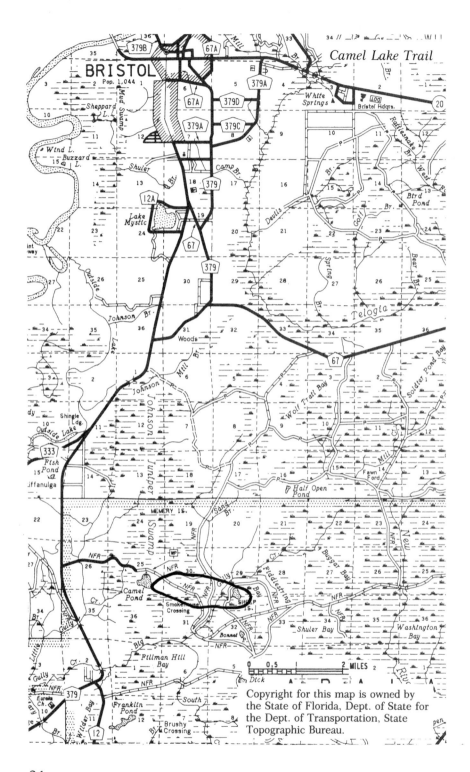

Camel Lake Trail

24

Coastal Trails of Northwest Florida

*Trails of the St. Joseph
  Peninsula*
T. H. Stone Memorial State
  Park
18 miles

St. George Island Trail
Dr. Julian G. Bruce State Park
3.5 miles

St. Vincent Island Trails
St. Vincent National Wildlife
  Refuge
96 miles

St. Marks Trails
St. Marks National Wildlife
  Refuge
  Stoney Bayou, 6 miles
  Deep Creek, 12 miles

Otter Lake Trails
St. Marks National Wildlife
  Refuge
  Ridge Trail, 4.6 miles
  Otter Lake, 7.9 miles

The St. Marks Trail
Apalachicola National Forest/
  St. Marks National Wildlife
  Refuge
45 miles

Trails of the St. Joseph Peninsula

T. H. Stone Memorial State Park
Gulf County (near Port St. Joe)
18 miles

St. Joseph Peninsula, a narrow spit of land 14 miles long, lies off the Gulf coast oriented in a north-south direction. It is connected to the mainland by an equally narrow natural causeway called Cape San Blas. The most northerly ten miles of the spit are owned by the state of Florida and make up T. S. Stone Memorial State Park and the St. Joseph Peninsula Wilderness Preserve.

Very large and beautiful sand dunes are found in the preserve, along with plant species indigenous to a salty environment: sea oats, sea purslane, and railroad vine. Behind the dunes, sand pine scrub, slash pine flatwoods, and freshwater marshes can be found.

Bird watching is excellent, especially during fall hawk migration. Reddish egrets and Wilson's and snowy plovers may be seen with the ubiquitous gulls and sandpipers. The limited accessibility of the beaches leads to good shelling as well.

The trail is nine miles, one-way, from the state park area to the end of the preserve. One may hike either on the Gulf beach, along the shore of St. Joseph Bay, or through fire lanes in the interior of the peninsula. The peninsula is never as much as a mile wide and the hiker is always within sight or sound of the Gulf. Camping is permitted behind the dunes but water is not available. Hikers must register with the ranger before setting out, as only 20 persons per day are allowed in the preserve.

Begin: At the ranger station at the state park.

End: Same place.

Camping: Primitive camping behind the dunes. Camping with all facilities is available at the state park.

Difficulty: Moderate.

For Further Information: Park Manager, T. H. Stone Memorial, St. Joseph Peninsula State Park, P.O. Box 909, Port St. Joe, FL 32456. (904) 227-1329

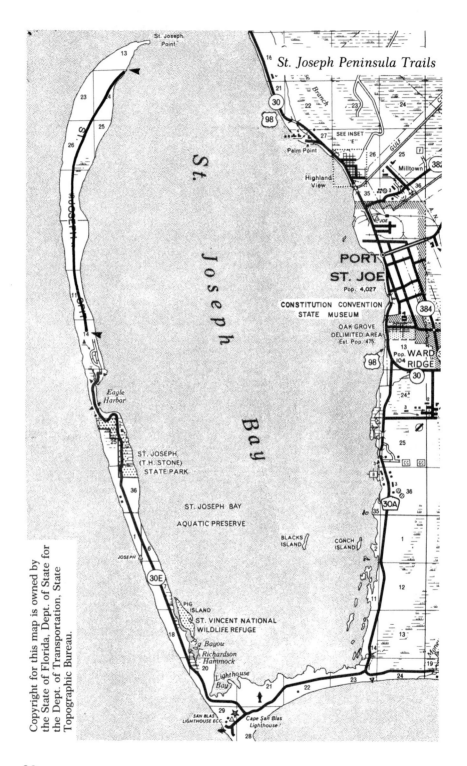

St. Joseph Peninsula Trails

St. George Island Trail

Dr. Julian G. Bruce St. George Island State Park
Franklin County (near Eastpoint)
3.5 miles

St. George Island is one of the few northern Florida barrier islands that can be reached by automobile. It lies off the coast in an east-west orientation and encloses Apalachicola Bay. The state owns 1,884 acres at the eastern end of the island that includes nine miles of beaches and dunes. Typical barrier island vegetation is seen there, including small forests of slash pine and scrub oak with some hammocks of oak and magnolia.

The hiking trail begins near Sugar Hill and follows the winding path of an old turpentine road to a primitive camping area at Gap Point, on the bay. One of the major reasons for hiking on St. George, other than to enjoy the unspoiled beaches, is to watch the birds. Winter birds include red-breasted nuthatch and dark-eyed junco, as well as the northern gannet, American oystercatcher, and common goldeneye. In addition, water pipits and vesper and savannah sparrows have been sighted. Experienced bird watchers say that Sprague's pipits can be seen here, along with as many as 33 species of warblers.

The island is reached by turning off US 98 onto county road G1A at Eastpoint and crossing the toll bridge.

Begin: At Sugar Hill Beach parking area.

End: Same place.

Camping: Primitive camping at Gap Point. Drinking water is available. Full facilities are available at the state park campground.

Difficulty: Easy.

For Further Information: Park Manager, Dr. Julian G. Bruce St. George Island State Park, P.O. Box 62, East Point, FL 32328. (904) 670-2111

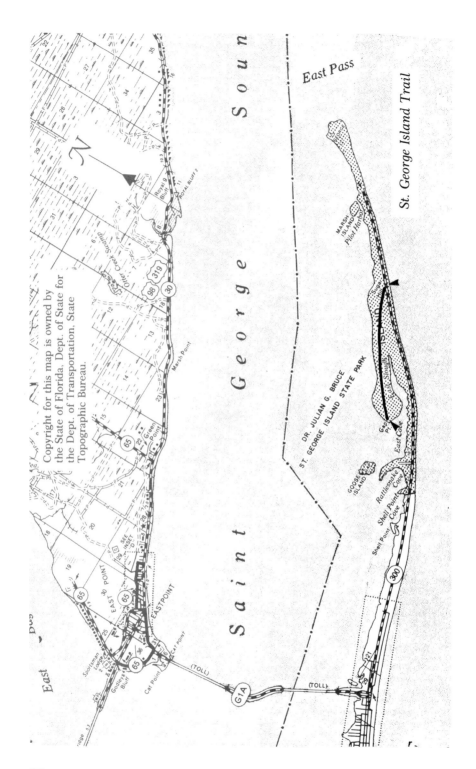

St. George Island Trail

East Pass

East Sou

George

Saint

East Pass

MARSH
ISLAND
Pilot Harbor

DR. JULIAN G. BRUCE

ST. GEORGE ISLAND STATE PARK

Gap Pt.

East Cove

GOOSE
ISLAND

Rattlesnake
Cove

Shell Point
Cove

Shell Point

300

21

(TOLL)

(TOLL)

G1A

Marsh Point

Royal Bluff

ROYAL BLUFF

Green
Point

65

65

98

319

30

Otter Creek Swamp

EAST POINT

EASTPOINT

65

65

65

CAT POINT

Cat Point

Sportsman
Lodge

Godley's
Bluff

East Pass

N

30

St. Vincent Island Trails

St. Vincent National Wildlife Refuge
Franklin County (near Apalachicola)
96 miles

St. Vincent Island is one of a chain of barrier islands located off the coast of Franklin County. It is separated from St. George Island by a very narrow pass on the eastern end, and from the mainland to the west, by an even slimmer strait. The island's history is quite interesting. It was used as a private hunting club from the early 1900s and the owners introduced many exotic species such as zebra, Sambur deer, and black buck. All but the Sambur deer have been removed, and they are seldom seen. Native wildlife on the island include white-tailed deer, turkey, and feral hogs.

St. Vincent is wider than most barrier islands and its terrain is more varied. It boasts not only Gulf beaches and dunes but also salt marshes, sizable freshwater ponds, and hardwood hammocks. Its size and inaccessibility account for the diversity of wildlife found there, and its seclusion makes it a bird watcher's paradise. Many, many species of shore birds, water birds, and wading birds may be seen in addition to the endangered bald eagle.

The island is shaped like a triangle some nine miles long and four miles wide at its broadest point. The 96 miles of trail consist of 16 miles of beach along the south shore and 80 miles of inland trail. The inland trails consist of seven or eight old east-west roads running roughly parallel to each other from the vicinity of West Pass to Indian Pass. These roads are interconnected with a number of north-south trails. The overall effect is that of a grid of trails over the entire island.

Since the island is a day-use area only and overnight camping is not allowed, it is necessary to return again and again to fully experience all that it has to offer. Transportation to the island can be arranged with fishing guides at Indian Pass or at Apalachicola. Indian Pass itself is easily navigated by canoe and there are several interesting trails at the west end of the island. This is an option for those who would like to explore without making a major commitment.

Begin: From either Indian Pass or West Pass. Foot trails lead into the interior and the shore trail leads to St. Vincent Point. Starting and ending points depend on where hikers embark on the island and where they have arranged to be picked up.

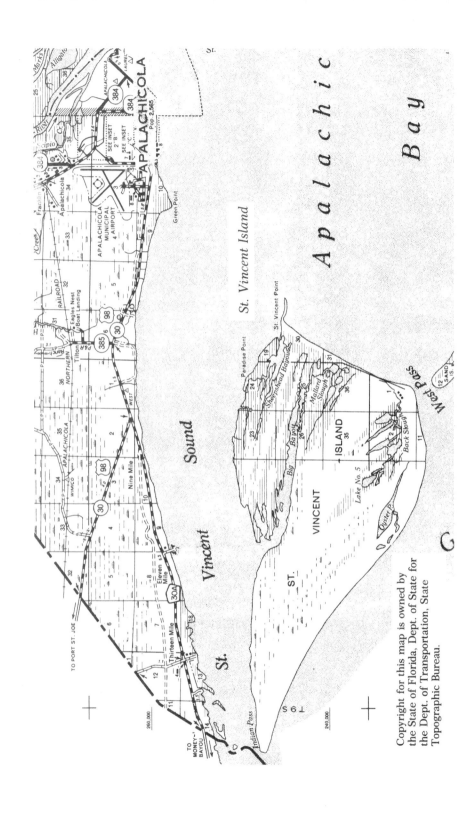

Camping: Not permitted.

Difficulty: Easy to moderate.

For Further Information: Refuge Manager, St. Marks National Wildlife Refuge, P.O. Box 68, St. Marks, FL 32355. (904) 925-6121

St. Marks Trails

St. Marks National Wildlife Refuge
Wakulla County (near St. Marks)
Stoney Bayou Trail: 6 miles
Deep Creek Trail: 12 miles

The St. Marks National Wildlife Refuge is one of the oldest in the National Wildlife Refuge system and is a magnificent example of a north Florida coastal environment. It contains 65,000 acres of land and 31,500 acres of water. This extremely diverse area includes freshwater impoundments, natural marshes, freshwater creeks, brackish bays, tidal flats, hardwood swamps, pine woods, and miles of shoreline. Over 17,000 acres are part of the National Wilderness system and are to be protected in their natural state. In addition, the State of Florida has recently purchased an adjoining 64,000 acres that extends public ownership of the Big Bend coastline from the refuge to the Suwannee River.

The area is of historical interest as well. Indian mounds that are over 2,000 years old can be found along the coast, and more recent sites of note include the West Goose Creek Seine Yard where seining for mullett has occurred for at least 150 years. Fort San Marcos de Apalachee, located in nearby St. Marks, was established in 1679 and has a colorful history. Salt vats, used by the Confederacy during the Civil War, are still visible in some of the salt marshes, and the St. Marks Lighthouse, built in 1831, is located at the end of county road 59 in the refuge.

Wildlife is abundant and includes Florida natives such as black bear, otter, raccoon, white-tailed deer, and an enormous population of American alligators. More than 300 species of birds have been reported from the refuge. Every hiker should get a copy of *Birds of St. Marks*, a pamphlet listing 272 species that are considered part of the refuge's fauna and 22 other species that are occasionally sighted.

Both the Stoney Bayou Trail and the Deep Creek Trail begin on county road 59 (Lighthouse Road) and follow rough service roads, dikes built to impound water, and abandoned railroad beds. The Deep Creek

Trail follows the roadbed of the old Aucilla Tram Road deep into a coastal swamp that will cause the hiker to expect Tarzan to swing by at any moment! The trail turns south and encircles East and West Stoney Bayou Pools and then returns via the impoundment dikes. The Stoney Bayou Trail is an abbreviated version of the same trail. Both are loop trails.

The refuge is a day-use area and no overnight camping is allowed. Hikers should stop at the visitor's center near the entrance to the refuge on county road 59; maps and other information—including the *Birds of St. Marks* booklet—are available there.

Begin: Off CR 59, south of the visitor's center.

End: Same place; these are loop trails.

Difficulty: Easy.

For Further Information: Refuge Manager, St. Marks National Wildlife Refuge, P.O. Box 68, St. Marks, FL 32355. (904) 925-6121

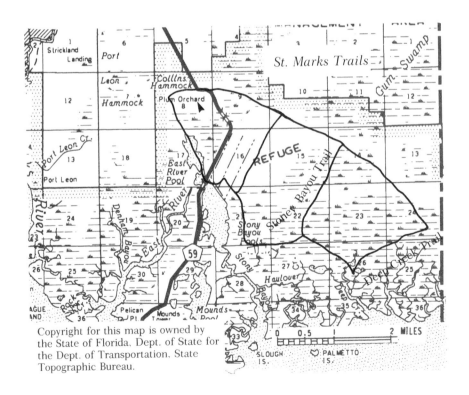

Copyright for this map is owned by the State of Florida, Dept. of State for the Dept. of Transportation, State Topographic Bureau.

Otter Lake Trails

St. Marks National Wildlife Refuge
Wakulla County (near Panacea)
Ridge Trail: 4.6 miles
Otter Lake Loop: 7.9 miles

Otter Lake Recreation Area is a part of the St. Marks National Wildlife Refuge located near Panacea. The lake is a favorite of nature lovers because of its secluded location and its large population of nesting ospreys. It also boasts an impressive population of American alligators.

The two trails utilize old forest roads and traverse forests of long-leaf pine and turkey oak, and an open field. The Loop Trail is marked with blue blazes, while the Ridge Trail is marked with yellow. Otter Lake is a day-use area and no camping is allowed. Picnic tables, restrooms, and potable water are available at the recreation area.

Begin: In Panacea, turn off US 98 onto CR 372A, which will lead to the Otter Lake Recreation Area. The trails begin just inside the refuge boundary.

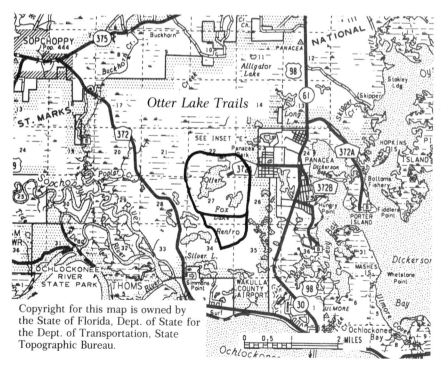

End: Same place; these are loop trails.

Difficulty: Easy.

For Further Information: Refuge Manager, St. Marks National Wildlife Refuge, P.O. Box 68, St. Marks, FL 32355. (904) 925-6121

The St. Marks Trail

Apalachicola National Forest/St. Marks National Wildlife Refuge
Wakulla, Jefferson counties (near St. Marks)
45 miles

The Florida Trail Association maintains a trail through the St. Marks Refuge. It begins at US 319 about five miles east of the town of Sopchoppy and continues to US 98, about 15 miles east of Newport. It occasionally crosses short sections of private property, but the refuge provides a map of the trail to the public and the staff there do not feel that access is a problem.

This is a very beautiful trail that offers a variety of hiking experiences. It begins at the point where the Apalachicola Trail ends in the Sopchoppy-Panacea area and is dry for most of the year. Points of interest include views of salt marshes in the Spring Creek area, Shepard Spring, the impoundments, freshwater marshes, the jungle-like terrain of the Aucilla Tram Road, the extremely beautiful and remote Pinhook River, and the hardwood swamps in the Aucilla River area. All of the refuge property is for day use only, so hikers should plan accordingly. Access points are at mile 8.2 (county road 365), and at mile 19 (US 98); the trail follows paved roads for several miles after the US 98 juncture with the refuge.

Begin: On US 319, east of Sopchoppy.

End: On US 98, east of Newport.

Camping: At Newport Division of Forestry Campground.

Difficulty: Easy to moderate.

For Further Information: Refuge Manager, St. Marks National Wildlife Refuge, P.O. Box 68, St. Marks, FL 32355. (904) 925-6121

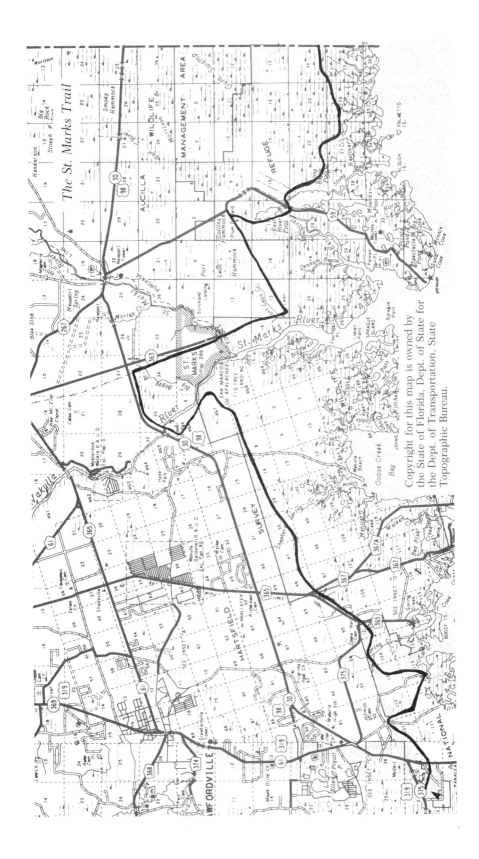

The St. Marks Trail

Copyright for this map is owned by the State of Florida, Dept. of State for the Dept. of Transportation, State Topographic Bureau.

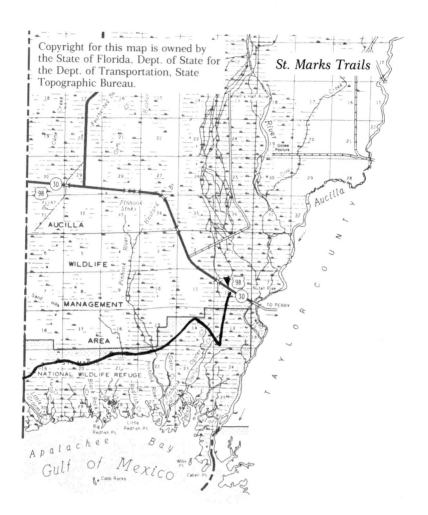

St. Marks Trails

Copyright for this map is owned by
the State of Florida, Dept. of State for
the Dept. of Transportation, State
Topographic Bureau.

Trails of North and Northeast Florida

Manatee Springs Trail
Manatee Springs State Park
3 miles

Natural Bridge Trail
O'Leno State Park
12 miles

Osceola Trail
Osceola National Forest
39 or 24 miles

Cary State Forest Trails
Cary State Forest
1 to 18 miles

Ft. Clinch Trail
Ft. Clinch State Park
6 miles

Island Hiking Trail
Little Talbot Island State Park
4.1 miles

Gold Head Branch Trail
Mike Roess, Gold Head
    Branch State Park
3 miles

Rice Creek Trail
Rice Creek Sanctuary
3 miles

Bulow Creek Trail
Bulow Plantation Ruins State
    Historic Site
4 miles

The Ocala Trail
Ocala National Forest
66 miles

Manatee Springs Trail

Manatee Springs State Park
Levy County (near Chiefland)
3 miles

Manatee Springs, on the Suwannee River, is one of Florida's loveli-
est natural areas. It is located in dense woods on the east side of the
river and produces a clear green pool framed by cypress and colorful
hardwoods. William Bartram described the spring on his 1774 journey
through Florida. The area supports an abundance of white-tailed deer,
raccoons, opossums, and other small mammals, as well as alligators and

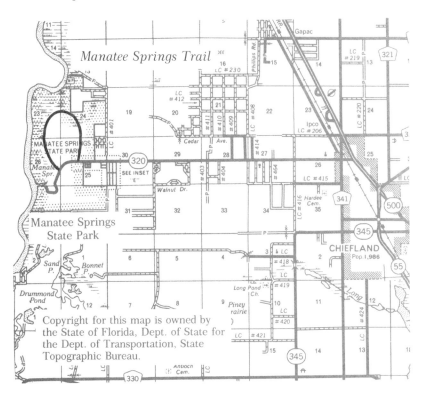

various types of wading birds. Watch for pileated woodpeckers near the river.

The trail is an unmarked loop that begins about one-quarter mile south of the entrance station to the park on the west side of the road. It follows the path of several old woods roads through a hammock of mixed hardwoods and pine. Several small ponds and some cypress swamp can be seen, but the trail itself is dry. Remember to keep to the left at each turning, as the hiker is always turning to the inside of the loop. It is necessary to check with the ranger before beginning your hike.

Begin: At Manatee Springs State Park, off SR 55, south of Chiefland. The trail head is one-quarter mile south of the park entrance station on the right.

End: On the same road two or three hundred yards further south. You will be able to see your vehicle parked at the entrance when you exit.

Camping: At the state park campground.

Difficulty: Easy.

For Further Information: Manatee Springs State Park, Rt. 2, Box 617, Chiefland, FL 32626. (904) 493-4288

Natural Bridge Hiking Trail

O'Leno State Park
Columbia, Alachua counties (near Lake City)
12 miles

This is one of Florida's most historic trails: it traverses the "natural bridge" of the Santa Fe River, a crossing point for path makers and road builders from earliest times. De Soto may have used it on his 1539 trip through Florida; Bellamy used it as part of his road from St. Augustine to Pensacola in the 1830s; and it was the site of the "wire road," the first telegraph line linking Florida with the outside world. A road or path is shown there on Tanner's 1823 map of Florida with the notation that "the creek is subterranean ... half a mile."

O'Leno itself is the site of a nineteenth-century town that once contained a mill, general store, hotel, and livery stable. Despite all of this early traffic, later road builders followed the railroads to the north and south of O'Leno and the area has now reverted to a unique and beautiful wilderness. The state park and the River Rise State Preserve encompass

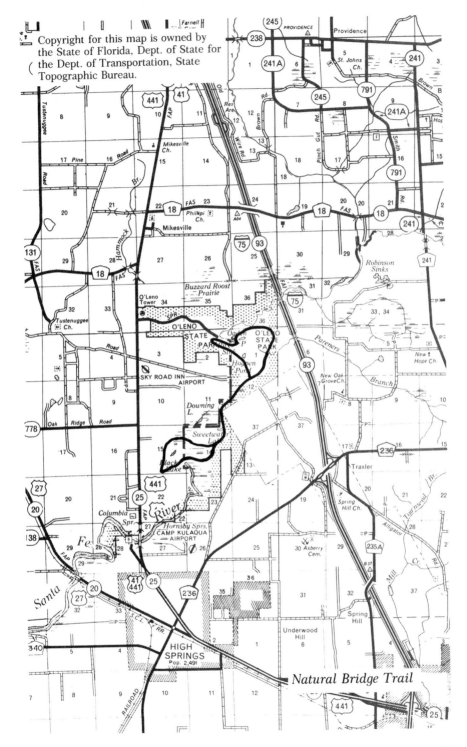

Natural Bridge Trail

43

the "river sink" where the Santa Fe River goes underground and the "river rise," where it comes up again, as well as 6,000 acres of sinkholes, hardwood hammocks, river swamp, and sandhill communities.

Wildlife in the park and preserve include raccoon, opossum, turkey, bobcat, and very tame deer. The deer love salty snacks, such as potato chips, and can be a real nuisance at mealtimes. The river swamps attract many varieties of migratory birds including the bald eagle. In summer, hooded warbler, Chuck-will's-widow and Mississippi kite may be seen.

The trail is laid out in a series of loops to give the hiker a change of scene. One may begin near the picnic/parking area and choose either the Wire Road or the River Sink route. After viewing the sink, hikers bound for the River Rise will continue on Pareners Branch Route to rejoin the Wire Road later. The Black Lake Route, another loop, crosses a swamp forest area and returns to the main trail below Sweetwater Lake. Primitive camping is available at Sweetwater Lake but is limited to 12 persons at one time. Hikers who plan to camp must register with the ranger and pay a small fee. Camping with full facilities is available at O'Leno State Park. Day hikers are encouraged to take the shorter walks on the River Sink and Pareners Branch trails. Note that although these trails are well marked, the brochure put out by the park may be confusing.

Begin: At O'Leno State Park, off US 41/441 south of Lake City.

End: Same place; this is a loop trail.

Camping: Primitive camping at Sweetwater Lake; full facilities at O'Leno State Park.

Difficulty: Easy.

For Further Information: O'Leno State Park, Rt. 2, Box 307, High Springs, FL 32543.

Butch Horn

Natural Bridge Hiking Trail, O'Leno State Park

Osceola Trail

Osceola National Forest
Columbia, Baker counties (near White Springs)
39 or 24 miles

This part of the Florida National Scenic Trail leaves Stephen Foster State Folk Culture Center near White Springs and travels, primarily by developed roads, to Olustee Battlefield Memorial in the Osceola National Forest. Although some of the first few miles of the trail are beside the Suwannee River, most of the remainder run along paved state roads and may not be of interest to most hikers. At mile 14.6 the trail enters the National Forest, and although it continues to follow old jeep roads, power lines, and railroad grades, it is still much more interesting. It leads through pine flatwoods as well as cypress and creek swamps— fine habitat for wildlife. Two endangered species occur here: red-cockaded woodpecker and gray bat. The many game animals making this their home include deer, turkey, and black bear. A number of small ponds along the way make pretty picnic stops and the wildflowers are most prominent in the spring.

The Olustee Memorial marks the site of a Civil War battle and provides a small museum of artifacts and exhibits from that era. Restrooms and potable water are available here. There are three approved campsites along the trail and water also is available at West Tower at mile 16.

Begin: At Stephen Foster Memorial off US 41 near White Springs, or at US 441 and NFR 262.

End: At Olustee Memorial in the Osceola National Forest off US 90 at Olustee.

Camping: On the trail or at Ocean Pond Campground off US 90 north of Olustee Memorial.

Difficulty: Easy.

For Further Information: District Ranger, U.S. Dept. of Agriculture Forest Service, Rt. 7, Box 95, Lake City, FL 32055. (904) 752-2577

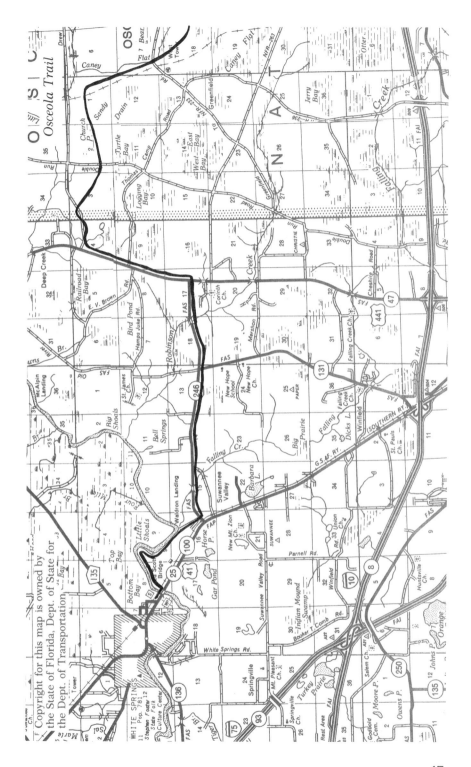

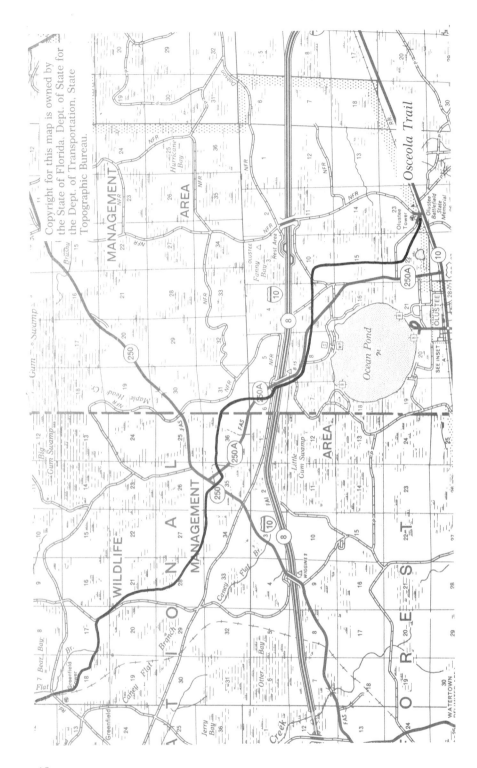

Cary State Forest Trails

Cary State Forest
Duval, Nassau counties (near Baldwin)
1 to 18 miles

This small state forest is little known but is a charming pocket wilderness only a few miles from bustling Jacksonville. One of its primary roles is providing environmental education activities for the Duval County schools and it is the site of many school field trips. It contains 3,411 acres of pine flatwoods, swamps, and wetlands, and an eight-acre borrow pit. Facilities include a pavilion, a bathhouse with showers, a camping area, fire tower, wildlife observation tower, several designated nature trails, and 18 miles of quiet forest roads suitable for hiking.

Wildlife in the forest include white-tailed deer, wild hogs, squirrels, raccoons, wild turkeys, bobcats, snakes, alligators, opossums, rabbits, and occasionally, a black bear. This is another area where local folk say the Florida panther still survives; but it has been many years since one has actually been sighted. Birds that are indigenous to pine flatwoods can be sighted here and include brown-headed nuthatch, pine warbler, Bachman's sparrow, yellow-throated vireo, and summer tanager.

Of particular interest is an extensive boardwalk trail built over the wet forest floor of a ti-ti swamp. Since this type of terrain is nearly impenetrable, hikers don't often get a chance to see it up close with so little effort!

Be sure to check with the ranger for up-to-the-minute information on the status of the trails and whether or not hunting activities are in progress. Ask for a map of the area.

Begin: Off US 301, about six miles north of Baldwin, at the parking area located near the main entrance of the state forest.

End: Same place; all trails loop and return to point of origin.

Camping: At the designated camping area.

Difficulty: Easy.

For Further Information: Cary State Forest, Fla. Division of Forestry, Jacksonville District, 8719 West Beaver Street, Jacksonville, FL 32220. (904) 693-5055)

Butch Horn

Hiking Trail, Cary State Forest

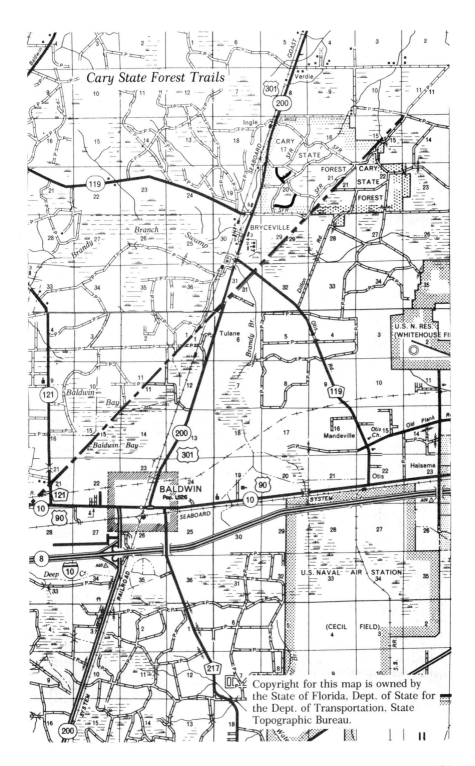

Cary State Forest Trails

Copyright for this map is owned by
the State of Florida, Dept. of State for
the Dept. of Transportation, State
Topographic Bureau.

51

Ft. Clinch Trail

Ft. Clinch State Park
Nassau County (near Fernandina Beach)
6 miles (round-trip)

Historic Ft. Clinch offers visitors entering Florida from the north
their first chance to go beachcombing. Located just across the St.
Mary's River from Georgia, this was one of several important Atlantic
fortifications. Huge sand dunes shelter the coastal hammock where the
campgrounds and picnic facilities are located.

The beach walk here is not a designated trail but is one that is frequently used by Boy Scouts as a part of their hiking badge requirements.
Beginning at the beach access just to the south of the fort and continuing
south to the state road A1A access in the city of Fernandina Beach, the
hiker traverses a distance of three miles. Marine life, such as sand crabs,

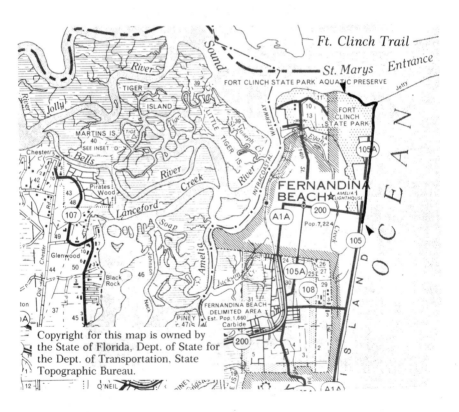

Copyright for this map is owned by
the State of Florida, Dept. of State for
the Dept. of Transportation, State
Topographic Bureau.

jelly fish, and assorted mussels, is more likely to be seen than any type of wildlife, but the bird watching can be excellent. Watch for wintering sparrows and purple sandpipers.

Begin: At the beach access just south of the fort.

End: Same place, or have someone pick you up at the SR A1A access in Fernandina Beach.

Camping: At the state park; all facilities are available.

Difficulty: Easy.

For Further Information: Ft. Clinch State Park, 2601 Atlantic Avenue, Fernandina Beach, FL 32034. (904) 277-7274

Butch Horn

Island Hiking Trail, Little Talbot Island

Island Hiking Trail

Little Talbot Island State Park
Duval County (near Jacksonville)
4.1 miles

Little Talbot Island is one of a series of Atlantic coastal islands that
are separated from the mainland by salt marshes and saltwater
creeks rather than by open water. On the Atlantic side, Little Talbot
boasts beautiful white sand beaches, while to the west, hammock vegetation and salt marshes predominate. The hiking trail begins on the west
side between the entrance gate and the entrance station to the state park
and is well marked. The trail passes through vegetation that is typical of
the landward side of dunes: a thicket of low-growing cedars, small
oaks, palms, myrtles, and sea grapes. Shore birds may be observed on
the beach where, during the spring and fall, many migratory birds are
present.

It is necessary to register with the ranger before undertaking even
this short hike.

Begin: Trail head is just off SR A1A, just beyond the Little Talbot
Island entrance gate, on the left.

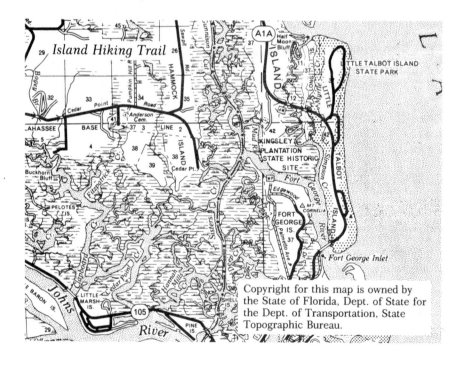

Copyright for this map is owned by
the State of Florida, Dept. of State for
the Dept. of Transportation, State
Topographic Bureau.

End: Same place; this is a "round-trip" trail.

Camping: At the state park; all facilities are available.

Difficulty: Easy.

For Further Information: Little Talbat Island State Pk., 12157 Heckschear Dr., Jacksonville, FL 32226. (904) 251-2320

Gold Head Branch Trail

Mike Roess, Gold Head Branch State Park
Clay County (Keystone Heights)
3 miles

Named for the very small quantities of gold that were once mined from this stream, Gold Head Branch provides a cool and refreshing change from the high sandhill scrub of the surrounding countryside. The stream meanders through a deep ravine canopied with a variety of hardwoods. The remains of an old mill can be seen. A 1.4-mile nature walk leads through the ravine and is a special treat on a hot summer day.

The Florida Trail Association maintains a 38-mile long trail through this area, three miles of which go through the state park. The remainder is on private property and open only to FTA members. The park section of trail begins just inside the entrance on the right, crosses Gold Head Branch via a bridge, and passes by the swimming area at Lake Johnson. This section is plainly marked with the FTA's orange blazes. The park also contains miles of woods roads that are suitable for hiking, but these are unmarked and require some orienteering skill.

Begin: At Gold Head Branch State Park, off SR 21 north of Keystone Heights. Just inside the entrance, look for the blazes on the left.

End: In the park, at the south boundary, less than one mile from the swimming area at Lake Johnson.

Camping: On the trail, at the designated primitive camping area, or at the state park campground.

Difficulty: Easy.

For Further Information: Gold Head Branch State Park, Rt. 1, Box 545, Keystone Heights, FL 32656. (904) 473-4701

Doug Sphar

Near Gold Head Branch State Park

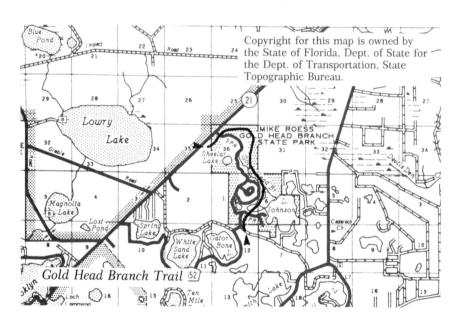

Gold Head Branch Trail 52

Rice Creek Trail

Rice Creek Sanctuary
Putnam County (near Palatka)
3 miles

The Rice Creek Sanctuary is located on private property owned by the Hudson Pulp and Paper Company but has been developed and maintained as a public facility. It is an area of historical significance since it is the site of a rice and indigo plantation dating from the time of the Revolutionary War. The dikes built to hold water for the rice paddies are still in existence.

The loop trail in the sanctuary has been designated a National Recreation Trail. It traverses pine flatlands and oak hammocks. There is a very pleasant picnic area at the entrance, but it is a day-use area only and camping is not allowed.

Begin: Off SR 100 about six miles west of Palatka.

End: Same place; this is a loop trail.

Difficulty: Easy.

For Further Information: Georgia Pacific Paper Company, P.O. Box 158, East Palatka, FL 32131. (904) 328-2796

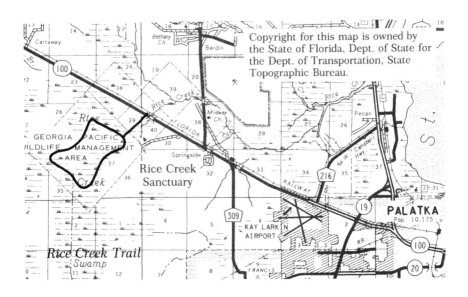

Copyright for this map is owned by the State of Florida, Dept. of State for the Dept. of Transportation, State Topographic Bureau.

Doug Sphar

Hiking out, Rice Creek Trail

Bulow Creek Trail

Bulow Plantation Ruins State Historic Site
Flagler, Volusia counties (near Flagler Beach)
4 miles

Bulow Creek is the site of a plantation started by Major Charles Bulow in 1821. At one time it consisted of almost 5,000 acres and was planted in sugar cane, cotton, rice, and indigo. It was abandoned during the Second Seminole War and was eventually burned by the Indians. John James Audubon visited in 1831 and described the plantation in his writings. The coquina ruins of the sugar mill and the foundation of the mansion can still be seen.

The primary attraction of the park to modern visitors are the very fine stands of live oak trees found there. Some of the trees are said to be over 200 years old. Not only do they provide a beautiful canopy for the hiker to enjoy, but they are a reminder of how many areas of Florida looked during territorial days. The trail follows the old plantation road, crosses a stream and an island, overlooks Marsh Point and returns via a waterfall that cascades over a limerock ledge.

Begin: The state historic site is located off CR 201, about five miles south of Flagler Beach. It is less than two miles from I-95 at exit 90 (Old Dixie Highway). The trail begins at the parking area.

End: Same place; this is a loop trail.

Camping: At nearby Flagler Beach State Park, on SR A1A a few miles south of Flagler Beach. Or, there is a private campground next to the park on Old Kings Highway.

Difficulty: Easy.

For Further Information: Bulow Plantation State Historic Site, P.O. Box 655, Bunnell, FL 32010. (904) 439-2219

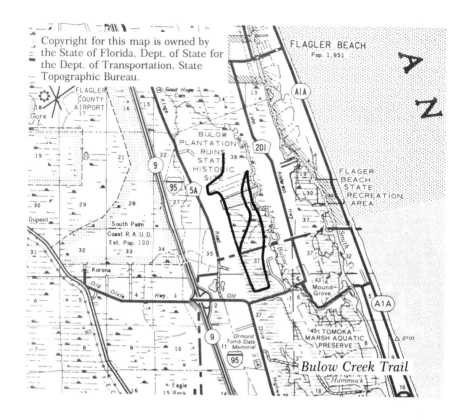

The Ocala Trail

Ocala National Forest
Lake, Marion counties (near Ocala)
66 miles

This is the longest section of continuous trail located on public property in Florida. It is contained entirely within the 366,000-acre Ocala National Forest and passes through a wide variety of terrain. Historically, it is said to have been part of the path traversed by Hernando de Soto in 1539. After leaving the Indian town of "Ocale" on August 11 of that year, he headed north toward "Apalachee." It had been a rainy summer and the traveling army was delayed by the necessity of constructing log bridges to cross the many streams. As you hike the trail, think of nearly 700 Spaniards, 233 horses and mules, a horde of domestic animals, and a bevy of Indian guides slogging along in the muggy August weather. Whatever your own condition, it is bound to make you feel better!

The forest primarily consists of slash pine, but these upland forests are dotted with many small ponds and swampy grass "prairies." There are also charming hardwood hammocks and near the river and stream beds, deep cypress-gum swamp can be found. In addition, "islands" of longleaf pine have been preserved for habitat for the endangered red-cockaded woodpecker.

Most small mammals common to north-central Florida can be found in the National Forest, and white-tailed deer are particularly abundant. Bird watchers should look for pine warbler, brown-headed nuthatch, Bachman's sparrow, scrub jay, and, of course, the red-cockaded woodpecker.

The northern terminus of the Ocala Trail is at Rodman Dam, with the southern terminus located at Clearwater Lake Campground. Since the trail frequently uses and/or crosses forest roads, it is easy to enter and exit at many points in between. The National Forest Service provides excellent maps and the trail is well marked. This also is part of the Florida Trail. Camping is permitted along the trail, though campers are asked to locate campsites at least 100 feet from it. During deer hunting season camping is permitted in designated sites only. Use of open fires is sometimes prohibited. It is always best to check with the District Ranger office for up-to-the-minute news on trail usage.

Begin: At Rodman Recreation Area, to travel north to south. From SR 19 drive west on NFR 77-1 for about five miles; turn right on NFR 88-4 and continue for about one mile; the trail blaze will be on the left.

End: At Clearwater Lake Campground. You may also wish to hike from south to north. In that case travel SR 19 to Altoona. Turn east on CR 42 and continue for about seven miles to Clearwater Lake.

Camping: There are eight campgrounds that are accessible by vehicle. Fees are charged at Clearwater Lake, Alexander Springs, and Juniper Springs. Camping is also permitted along the trail except during hunting season (check with the ranger for regulations).

Difficulty: Easy to moderate.

For Further Information: Ocala Trail, Ocala National Forest, Visitor's Center, 10863 Highway 40, Silver Springs, FL 32688.

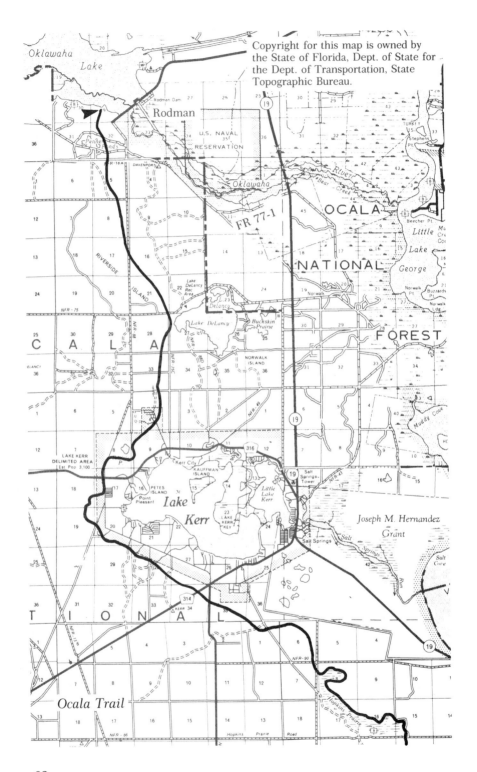

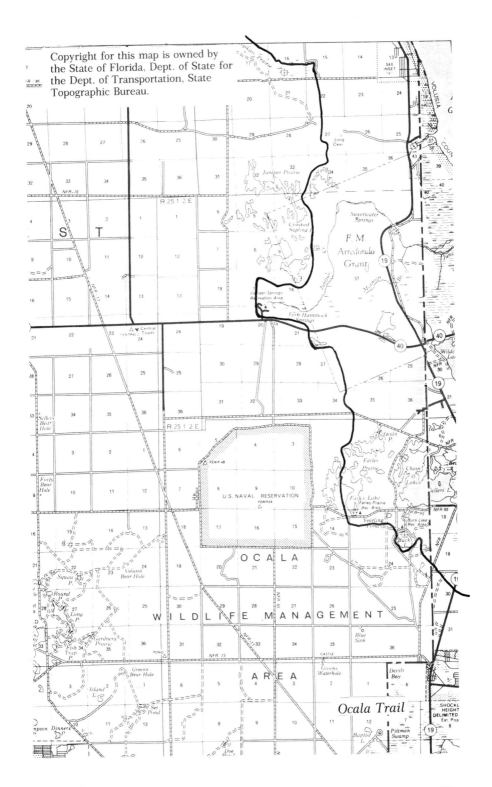

63

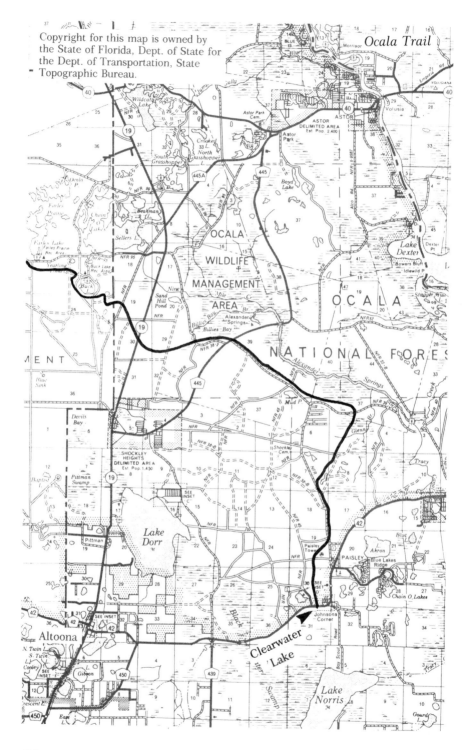

Ocala Trail

64

Trails of Central Florida

Withlacoochee Trails
Withlacoochee State Forest
  Citrus, 40.6 miles
  Croom, 22.3
  Richloam, 24.9
  Colonel Robins, 3.2
  McKethan Lake, 2.5

Wekiwa Springs Trail
Wekiwa Springs State Park
13.5 miles

Tosohatchee Trails
Tosohatchee State Reserve
  Outer Loop, 17 miles
  Entire Trail, 27 miles

Sand Road Trail
Canaveral National Seashore
13 miles

Beach Trail
Canaveral National Seashore
24 miles

*Max Hoeck Creek Wildlife
  Drive*
Canaveral National Seashore
4.3 miles

Merritt Island Refuge Trails
Merritt Island National
  Wildlife Refuge
  Blackpoint Wildlife Drive, 7
  miles
  *Allan Cruickshank Memorial
  Trail*, 5 miles

Prairie Lakes Trails
Prairie Lakes State Preserve
  North Loop, 5.5 miles
  South Loop, 5.7 miles

Lake Kissimmee Trails
Lake Kissimmee State Park
  North Loop Trail, 6.1 miles
  Buster Island Loop, 6.4
  miles
  Gobbler Ridge Trail, 4.2
  miles

Lake Arbuckle Trail
Avon Park Air Force Base
16 miles

Withlacoochee Trails

Withlacoochee State Forest
Pasco, Hernando, Citrus counties

The Withlacoochee State Forest comprises 113,431 acres in four separate tracts. Each area has its own unique characteristics, with the Withlacoochee River being the thread that links them together. Three of the four areas contain extensive trail systems that are part of the Florida Trail. It is an area rich in natural resources and in history. De Soto is known to have passed through the area in 1539 and recent archaeological finds have placed his entourage at a site along US 41 near Inverness. The major battles of the Second Seminole War were also fought in these pine woods.

Citrus Hiking Trail

Withlacoochee State Forest
Citrus County (near Inverness)
46.1 miles

The Citrus area is noted for its high, rolling sandhills that are covered with scrub oaks and pines. Occasional hardwood hammocks, limestone sinkholes, and several small ponds are here as well. Wildlife that may be encountered include deer, fox, raccoon, and the unusual fox squirrel. Bird watchers should be alert for red-tailed hawks and quail. In the Stage Pond section of the trail, wood ducks and various migrant birds may be observed.

The trail consists of four loops, each with interconnecting trails. Thus, it is possible to hike from 8.5 miles on a single loop, to the full 40.6 miles of the entire trail. The trail is blazed with blue marks and may be closed during certain weeks of the hunting season. There are three designated campsites: at Holder Mine, at Perryman Place, and at the Mutual

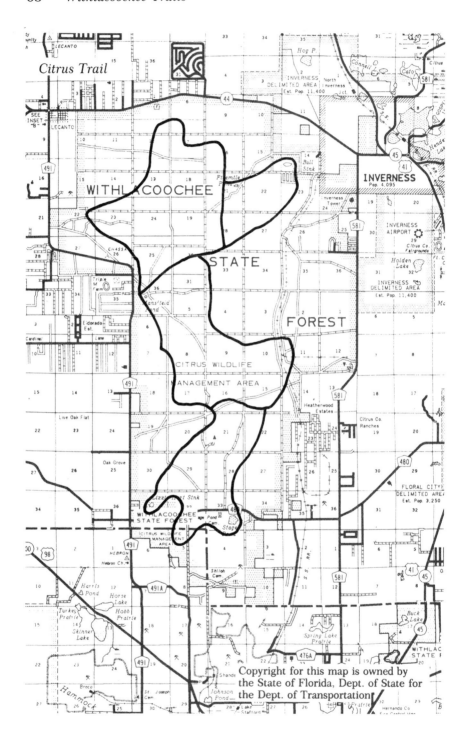

Citrus Trail

Mines Recreation Area. There are also two "camping zones" on the trail that are indicated by six-inch white bands painted on trees at eye level. Potable water is available at the recreation areas. Maps and other information may be obtained from the Division of Forestry. Since the area is laced with forest roads, it is essential to have a trail map before setting forth.

Begin: At Holder Mine Recreation Area, just off CR 581 about three miles south of Inverness.

End: Back at Holder Mine if you hike the entire trail. There are numerous access points including Mutual Mines Recreation Area, which is also off CR 581.

Camping: At Holder Mine Recreation Area, at Perryman Place, at Mutual Mines Recreation Area, and at the camp zones on the trail.

Difficulty: Easy to moderate.

For Further Information: Forest Supervisor's Office, Withlacoochee Forestry Center, 15019 Broad Street, Brooksville, FL 33601.

Croom Hiking Trail

Withlacoochee State Forest
Hernando County (near Brooksville)
31.3 miles

The Croom Trail is similar to the Citrus Trail in that it traverses high sandy hills covered with scrub oaks and pines. It is nearer to the Withlacoochee River, however, and as a result passes by more hardwood hammocks and cypress ponds. There are two deep ravines as well as a prairie and an abandoned rock mine that lend additional interest. The trail begins at the Silver Lake Recreation Area and follows the river for the first mile. There are three loops, all blazed with blue marks. Camping zones are identified by the six-inch white bands painted on trees at eye level.

This trail may be closed during certain weeks of the hunting season. Since the area is laced with forest roads, it is essential to have maps and other information before setting forth.

Begin: At Silver Lake Recreation Area. From Brooksville, travel east on SR 700 for about 10 miles until it passes under I-75; turn north (left) on the next paved road after passing under the interstate and continue to the Recreation Area.

End: Same place; this is a loop trail.

Camping: At Silver Lake Recreation Area and in the designated camping zones on the trail.

Difficulty: Easy.

For Further Information: Forest Supervisor's Office, Withlacoochee Forestry Center, 15019 Broad Street, Brooksville, FL 33601.

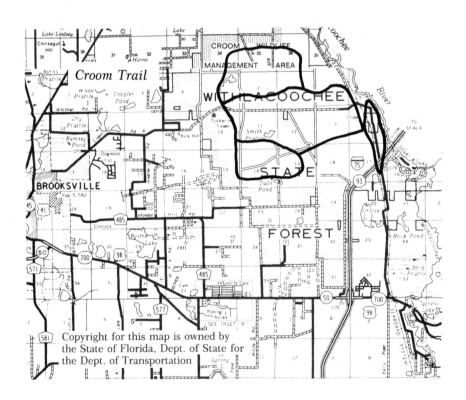

Copyright for this map is owned by the State of Florida, Dept. of State for the Dept. of Transportation

Richloam Hiking Trail

Withlacoochee State Forest
Pasco, Hernando counties (near Dade City)
31.5 miles

The Richloam Trail, as its name suggests, traverses deeper hardwood forests and more river swamps than the other Withlacoochee trails. As a result, it is wetter and care should be taken when hiking in the rainy season. It follows the Withlacoochee River for several miles in the southern section, borders the Little Withlacoochee River in the northern section, and crosses many small creeks and streams. The terrain varies from pine flatwoods, to hardwood hammocks, to cypress ponds. Several endangered species are indigenous to this area of the forest, including the red-cockaded woodpecker and the eastern indigo snake. Other natives are raccoon, bobcat, opossum, skunk, rabbit, deer, turkey, quail, and feral hogs. Bald eagles have been sighted here as well.

Also of interest to hikers of this trail are the herds of "cracker" ponies and the unusual cattle resembling longhorns, which may be observed grazing on some of the pastures along the way. The ponies are the offspring of horses used by the Florida cattlemen of the 1800s and are direct descendants of horses brought to Florida by Spanish explorers in the early 1500s. The cattle are also relics of that era—descendants of the Andalusian cattle that accompanied the early Spanish settlers.

The Richloam Trail is blazed with orange and is closed during the first nine days of hunting season as well as on Thanksgiving, Christmas, and New Year's holidays. Hikers also should be alert to the presence of hunters during the spring gobbler hunt. Camping is permitted at Megg's Hole and South Grade Barrow Pit as well as in the designated camping zones (marked by white-banded trees). Water may be obtained at Richloam Tower and at Megg's Hole.

Begin: At the Richloam Tower. From Dade City, travel north on US 98/SR 700 for about five miles to the village of Lacoochee; turn right (east) on SR 575 and continue to the intersection with SR 50; turn right (east) and travel for two miles to the Richloam Tower Road (SFR 9); turn right (south) and continue to the tower.

End: Same place; this is a loop trail.

Camping: At Megg's Hole, South Barrow Pit, or in the designated camping zones on the trail. There is an improved campground with all facilities at nearby Silver Lake Recreation Area.

Difficulty: Moderate.

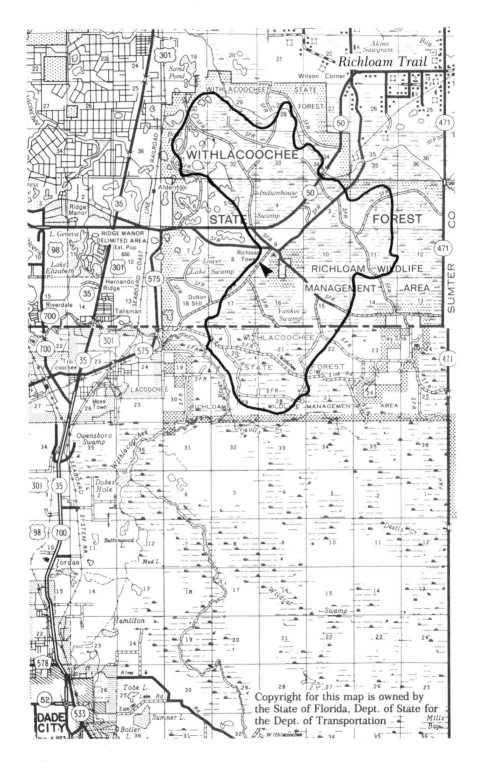

For Further Information: Forest Supervisor's Office, Withlacoochee Forestry Center, 15019 Broad Street, Brooksville, FL 33601.

Colonel Robins Trail

Withlacoochee State Forest
Hernando County (near Brooksville)
3.2 miles

This pleasant trail is located in a small, 2,000-acre outholding of the
state forest. It has been under government management since the
1930s and provides a fine example of southern pine flatwoods undergo-
ing the process of natural succession to hardwood forest. The trail is
marked with orange blazes and begins at a picnicking and recreation
area. This is a day-use area only.

Begin: At the Colonel Robins Recreation Area, located six miles
north of Brooksville off US 41.

End: Same place; this is a loop trail.

Camping: Not available.

Difficulty: Easy.

For Further Information: Same as below.

McKethan Lake Nature Trail

Withlacoochee State Forest
Hernando (near Inverness)
2.5 miles (lake road plus nature trail)

This charming trail is included because it is so beautiful, so accessible, and has such a wide variety of scenery in such a short distance.
The 1.5-mile trail around McKethan Lake is also an exercise course.
After completing it, the hiker can then traverse the mile-long nature trail
that goes through bottomlands, hardwood hammocks with lovely old canopy oaks, magnolias, and gum trees, and through pinelands that boast
four species of southern pine. The wildflowers are especially notable in
this area, and the lake is host to many varieties of wading and migratory

birds. The information pamphlet that accompanies the nature trail provides an excellent introduction to the types of trees that are common to this part of Florida.

Begin: At McKethan Lake Recreation Area, located about 12 miles south of Inverness off US 41.

End: Same place; this is a loop trail.

Difficulty: Easy.

For Further Information: Forest Supervisor's Office, Withlacoochee State Forest, 15023 Broad Street, Brooksville, FL 33512.

Butch Horn

McKethan Lake Nature Trail

Wekiwa Springs Trail

Wekiwa Springs State Park
Orange County (near Apopka)
13.5 miles

Wekiwa Springs are located in a beautiful semitropical forest not far
from Orlando. The springs are the headwaters, along with Rock
Springs, for the Wekiva River, which runs into the St. Johns. The entire
area has been left much as it was when Indians lived nearby, some 150
years ago. The trail was built by the Florida Trail Association and is
blazed in blue and white. It traverses a high sandy ridge, river swamp,
pine flatwoods, wet hammocks, and sand pine scrub. Other unusual terrain visited by this trail includes sinkholes—funnel-shaped depressions
in the ground—and bayheads, wet places where ground water seeps to
the surface. The trail also crosses several spring-fed streams and skirts
the beautiful Rock Springs Run. Animals indigenous to the area include
deer, fox squirrels, raccoons, rabbits, bobcats, foxes, and even bear.
Endangered species that may be seen are the eastern indigo snake and
the gopher tortoise.

"Wekiwa" or "Wekiva" is an Indian name meaning "a spring of
water." The state park uses what is considered the correct spelling

according to the Indian alphabet. The river and the state road are spelled "Wekiva" on official maps.

There are two designated campsites that will accommodate a limited number of people. Campers must register with the ranger. Potable water is available at the state park headquarters. Water obtained on the trail must be treated before drinking.

Begin: At Wekiwa Springs State Park. From Apopka, travel east on SR 436 to Wekiva Road; turn north and follow the signs to the park.

End: Same place; this is a loop trail.

Camping: In designated campsites on the trail. Camping with all facilities is available at the state park.

Difficulty: Easy.

For Further Information: Wekiwa Springs State Park, 1800 Wekiwa Circle, Apopka, FL 32703.

Wekiwa Springs Trail

Doug Sphar

Along the trail at Wekiwa Springs State Park

Tosohatchee Trails

Tosohatchee State Reserve
Orange County (near Orlando)
Outer Loop: 17 miles
Entire Trail: 27 miles

The Tosohatchee State Reserve borders 19 miles of the St. Johns River and is a beautiful and secluded wilderness located within a few miles of Orlando. It contains 28,000 acres of floodplain marshes, pine flatwoods, and hardwood hammocks. Several Indian mounds and the remains of an early cattle ranch occur here as well. Wildlife is varied and abundant and includes white-tailed deer, bobcat, gray fox, turkey, hawks, owls, and many types of song and wading birds. Endangered species such as black bear and bald eagle have also been seen in the reserve.

The trails here were blazed by the Florida Trail Association; they tend to follow primitive roads and artificially filled areas but may be wet during the rainy season. There are two primitive campsites with fire rings but no potable water. Campers are limited to 15 and both hikers and campers must register with the ranger before setting forth.

Begin: At Tosohatchee State Reserve, located about 20 miles south and east of Orlando off SR 50. Travel on SR 50 to the town of Christmas; turn right (south) on Taylor Creek Road and drive for about three miles to the entrance to the Reserve.

End: Same place; this is a loop trail.

Camping: Permitted on the trail with permission of the ranger.

Difficulty: Easy to moderate.

For Further Information: Tosohatchee State Reserve, Rt. 4, Box 812, Orlando, FL 32807.

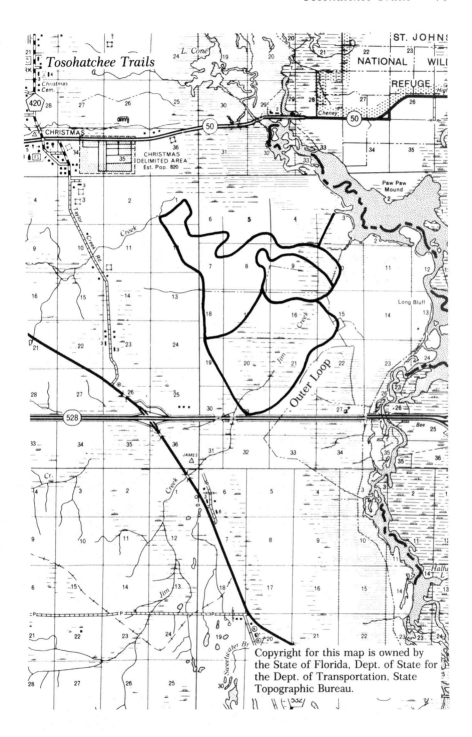

Sand Road Trail

Canaveral National Seashore
Volusia, Brevard counties (near Titusville)
13 miles

This trail is a two-rut road that runs behind the dunes along the Atlantic Ocean, from Apollo Beach to Parking Area #13 at Playalinda Beach. Vegetation peculiar to coastal dunes can be observed as well as the threatened eastern indigo snake and an abundance of rodents and insects. The primary attraction for the hiker is the wide variety of bird life that may be present. The Atlantic Flyway, a major migratory route for birds, passes overhead and is used by hundreds of thousands of birds on their journey north and south. There is no potable water available along the trail and crossing over the dunes to the ocean is not permitted.

Camping is allowed from Apollo Beach to the Volusia/Brevard county line, a distance of eight or nine miles. Camping and/or overnight hiking is not permitted from the Brevard county line to Playalinda Beach. Camping is also restricted during the turtle nesting season (May 15 to September 15) and during certain launch activities at the nearby Kennedy Space Center. Camping permits should be obtained from the visitor's center at Apollo State Park, at which time the ranger will advise of any prohibitions.

Begin: At Apollo Beach Visitor's Center, 12 miles south of New Smyrna Beach on SR A1A. The headquarters contact trailer is located 7 miles east of Titusville on CR 402.

End: At parking area #13 at Playalinda Beach, east of Titusville off CR 402.

Camping: On the trail from Apollo Beach to the Volusia/Brevard county line, when permitted. Check with the ranger.

Difficulty: Easy.

For Further Information: District Ranger's Office, Canaveral National Seashore, 308 Julia St., Titusville, FL 32796.

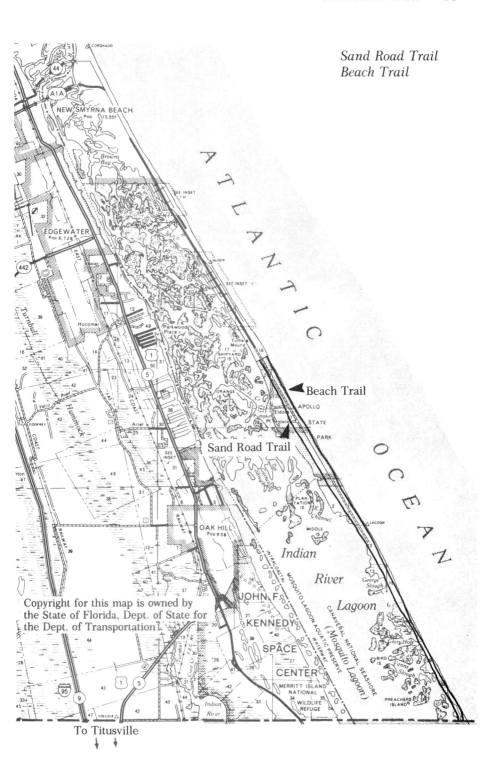

Sand Road Trail
Beach Trail

Beach Trail

Sand Road Trail

Copyright for this map is owned by
the State of Florida, Dept. of State for
the Dept. of Transportation.

To Titusville

Beach Trail

Canaveral National Seashore
Volusia, Brevard counties (near Titusville)
24 miles

This is one of the longest and most accessible stretches of publicly owned beach in Florida and provides a wonderful opportunity to experience the kind of "beachcombing" that was well known to our ancestors, but which now is almost a thing of the past.

While this particular beach is to the north of the route of the famous "Barefoot Mailmen," it is probably similar to the type of "hike" that these dedicated public servants made as they covered over 7,000 miles each year. The original "Barefoot Mailman" hiked from Palm Beach to Miami—a 100-mile stretch of beach along a wild and roadless coast. Today, the beach between Palm Beach and Miami is anything but wild and roadless, so enjoy this stretch instead.

Hikers are not allowed to cross the dunes to the Sand Road Trail and there is no potable water available. Camping and overnight hiking is permitted only from Apollo Beach to the Volusia/Brevard county line, a distance of eight or nine miles. Camping is restricted during the turtle nesting season and during certain launching activities at nearby Kennedy Space Center. Camping permits must be obtained from the ranger, who will advise of any prohibitions. In addition, hikers should be alert to the hazards of rough surf and high tides, especially when camping.

Begin: At Apollo Beach, located 12 miles south of New Smyrna Beach on SR A1A. The headquarters contact trailer is located 7 miles east of Titusville on CR 402.

End: At Playalinda Beach, parking area #13, east of Titusville off CR 402.

Camping: On the trail from Apollo Beach to the Volusia/Brevard county line only, and only during permitted times. Register with the ranger.

Difficulty: Easy.

For Further Information: District Ranger's Office, Canaveral National Seashore, 308 Julia St., Titusville, FL 32796.

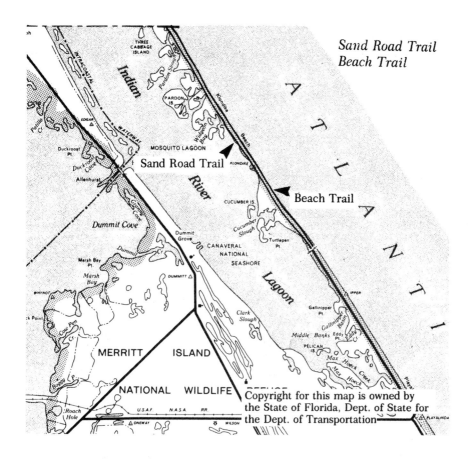

Sand Road Trail
Beach Trail

Max Hoeck Creek Wildlife Drive

Canaveral National Seashore
Brevard County (near Titusville)
4.3 miles

This trail is an auto tour that runs beside a railroad embankment through an impounded marsh. It is one-way for vehicles, beginning at the Playalinda Beach Road, so hikers should walk east from behind the Canaveral National Seashore Visitor's Center toward the beach. The advantages of hiking the drive are numerous. Several roads that branch off the drive are closed to vehicles but readily available to those on foot. Furthermore, there are not many places for vehicles to pull off the road to enjoy the scenery, and the bird watching is excellent. This area is under the Atlantic Flyway, a major migratory route for birds, and the marshes and impoundments along the drive provide excellent feeding/resting habitat for many species.

Begin: Behind the Canaveral National Seashore Visitor's Center, off CR 402.

End: At Playalinda Beach Road.

Camping: Not available.

Difficulty: Easy.

For Further Information: District Ranger's Office, Canaveral National Seashore, 308 Julia St., Titusville, FL 32796.

Merritt Island Refuge Trails

Merritt Island National Wildlife Refuge
Brevard County (near Titusville)
Black Point Wildlife Drive: 7 miles
Allan Cruickshank Memorial Trail: 5 miles

The Black Point Wildlife Drive is an auto tour that can also be enjoyed by hikers. It is especially recommended for those unfamiliar with coastal salt marsh, since it provides a quick lesson in what to be aware of in this type of terrain. The sand and shell road follows mosquito-

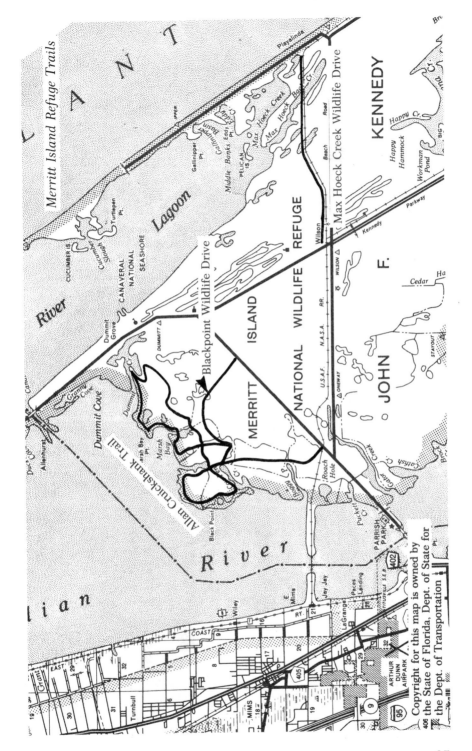

control dikes through the marshlands, passing mud flats, shallow water impoundments, and some pine flatland. The primary attraction here is birds. The refuge provides homes for more than 285 species and wintering areas for 28 types of migratory waterfowl. There are also 25 kinds of mammals, 117 fishes, and 65 types of amphibians and reptiles in the area.

The Allan Cruickshank Memorial Trail is reached from the Black Point Wildlife Drive and is named after the famous wildlife photographer, writer, and naturalist who was instrumental in the establishment of the refuge. Closed to vehicular traffic, the trail loops around Black Point Marsh, offering a unique view of three different types of habitats. Black Point hosts the convergence of salt marsh, marsh stream, and interior impoundment. An observation tower is located a short distance from the trail head. Trails in the National Wildlife Refuge are for day use only.

Begin: Blackpoint Wildlife Drive is located off SR 406 north of Titusville. The Allan Cruickshank Memorial Trail is located at Point #8 on the Black Point Wildlife Drive.

End: Both are loop trails.

Camping: Not available.

Difficulty: Easy.

For Further Information: Merritt Island National Wildlife Refuge, P.O. Box 6504, Titusville, FL 32782.

Prairie Lakes Trails

Prairie Lakes State Preserve
Osceola County (near St. Cloud)
North Loop: 5.5 miles
South Loop: 5.7 miles

The Prairie Lakes State Preserve is part of a very remote and isolated 50,000-acre area that is managed by the Florida Game and Freshwater Fish Commission. The preserve itself is not large, but it borders the sprawling Three Lakes Wildlife Management Area and Lake Kissimmee. The area is part of the Osceola Plain and its pinelands are dotted with small lakes, marshes, and hardwood hammocks. The preserve is not open for hunting and as a result supports a rich variety of wildlife. Birds are abundant and include the bald eagle and sandhill crane along with many other wading and shore birds.

The preserve contains two loop trails that are part of the Florida Trail Association's Prairie Lakes Section. Camping is permitted at two designated primitive campsites and there are pitcher pumps available. Hikers who plan to camp must register with the ranger in advance.

Begin: At Prairie Lakes State Preserve, located about 30 miles south of St. Cloud, off CR 523 (also called Canoe Creek Road).

End: Same place; these are loop trails.

Camping: On the trail at designated campsites. Advance registration is required.

Difficulty: Easy.

For Further Information: Superintendent, Prairie Lakes State Preserve, P.O. Box 220, Kenansville, FL 32739. (407) 436-1818

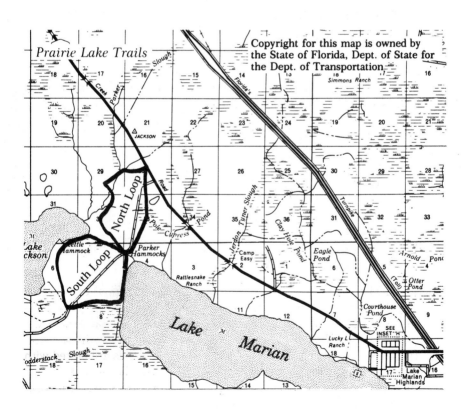

Doug Sphar

Marshes, Merritt Island National Wildlife Refuge

Doug Sphar

Giant oak on Prairie Lakes State Preserve

Lake Kissimmee Trails

Lake Kissimmee State Park
Polk County (near Lake Wales)
North Loop Trail: 6.1 miles
Buster Island Loop: 6.4 miles
Gobbler Ridge Trail: 4.2 miles

The area around Lake Kissimmee is called the Osceola Plain and is characterized by the large lake and an accompanying chain of smaller lakes, scrubby flatwoods, pinelands, hardwood hammocks, and wet prairies. This diversity of natural communities makes for interesting trails that meander through fine examples of central Florida "wilderness" terrain. It also provides a home for a variety of wildlife, including white-tailed deer, turkey, bobwhite, grey squirrel, fox squirrel, and bobcat. Song birds, wading birds, ospreys and sandhill cranes are often seen, and this is yet another area where the Florida panther is rumored to be still extant.

The trails here were built with the cooperation of the Florida Trail Association and are blazed in white. There are two primitive campsites on the trail but no potable water. Registration with the ranger is required of all hikers. The rangers at Lake Kissimmee are proud of their park and offer a wealth of information, both printed and oral, that is very useful to the visitor.

Begin: At Lake Kissimmee State Park, 17 miles east of Lake Wales off Camp Mack Road (CR 17B).

End: Same place; two are loop trails and the third is a round-trip trail.

Camping: Primitive camping on the trail. All facilities are provided at the state park.

Difficulty: Easy.

For Further Information: Lake Kissimmee State Park, 14248 Camp Mack Road, Lake Wales, FL 33853. (813) 696-1112

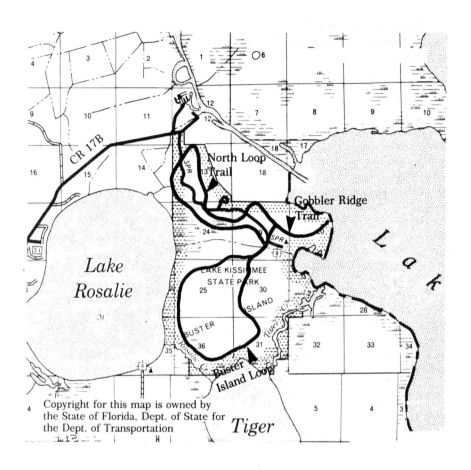

Lake Arbuckle Trail

Avon Park Air Force Base
Polk County (near Avon Park)
16 miles

This National Recreation Trail is located on the Avon Park Air Force
Base. It is open to the public but hikers must contact the Resource
Manager to register and to get information about any prohibitions or lim-
itations.

The trail covers terrain that is characteristic of central Florida, with
pine flatwoods being its primary feature. There are also some hardwood

hammocks and marsh areas. The site of Fort Arbuckle, one of the many fortifications built during the Seminole Wars, can be seen along the trail. This is a loop trail with a designated campsite at the access.

Begin: At the Avon Park Air Force Base, off CR 64, about ten miles east of Avon Park.

End: Same point; this is a loop trail.

Camping: At Willingham Campsite, at the beginning of the trail.

Difficulty: Easy.

Note: Do not hike on this trail without permission of the resource manager and the security police.

For Further Information: Natural Resources, 56 SS-CEN, 236 S. Boulevard, Avon Park, FL 33825 (813) 452-4119

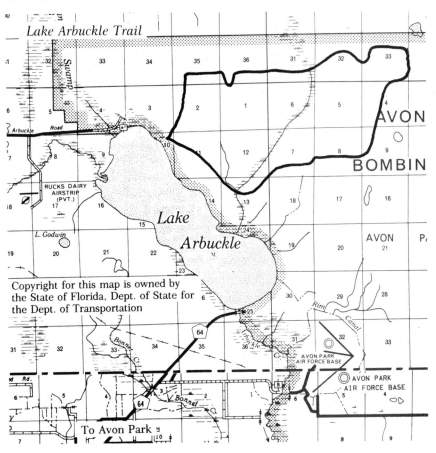

Doug Sphar

Old oak along the trail in Lake Kissimmee State Park

Trails of South Florida

Jonathan Dickinson Trail
Jonathan Dickinson State Park
7.8 miles

Marsh Nature Trail
Loxahatchee National Wildlife
  Refuge
3.2 miles

"Spite Highway"
Biscayne National Park
  North, 5 miles
  South, 9 miles

Trails of the Everglades
Everglades National Park
Royal Palm Area
  Slash Pine, 7 miles
  Loop Trail, 3 or 5 miles
  Old Ingraham Highway, 11
  miles
Flamingo Area
  Snake Bight, 4 miles
  Rowdy Bend, 5 miles
  Bear Lake, 4 miles
  Christian Point, 4 miles
  Coastal Prairie, 12 miles
  Alligator Creek, 14.6 miles
Shark Valley Area
  Tram Road, 15 miles

Big Cypress Trail, South
Big Cypress National Preserve
27 miles

Fakahatchee Strand Trail
Fakahatchee Strand State
  Preserve
10 miles

Collier-Seminole Trail
Collier-Seminole State Park
6.6 miles

Myakka Trail
Myakka River State Park
38 miles

Sanibel-Captiva Trail
Sanibel-Captiva Conservation
  Center
4.15 miles

Jonathan Dickinson Trail

Jonathan Dickinson State Park
Martin County (near Jupiter Island)
7.8 miles

Jonathan Dickinson, his wife, and their infant child were early Florida hikers although they had not planned to be. They were with a group of Quakers who were shipwrecked in the vicinity in 1696. After great difficulty, they eventually reached St. Augustine where they were able to arrange transportation to their home in Philadelphia. Mr. Dickinson's journal of their travails gives a valuable picture of life in early Florida. When you hike the trail, think of this little family, accompanied by a baby and without "state-of-the-art" camping and hiking gear, making their way to St. Augustine.

The state park is located on the banks of the Loxahatchee River, which has recently been designated a National Wild and Scenic River. The river is of historic interest as well, since it was near here that the Battle of Loxahatchee River took place on January 24, 1838. This was one of the many skirmishes of the Second Seminole War.

In all, the park encompasses over 10,000 acres of sand pine scrub, pine flatwoods, mangrove, and river swamp. The trail, which was built by the Florida Trail Association, winds through these plant communities and along Kitching Creek. It can be wet during the rainy season. There is a designated camping area on the trail with a pitcher pump well. Camping is limited to no more than eight persons and water from the pumps must be treated for drinking. Cooking fuel must also be packed in since firewood gathering is not allowed.

Begin: At Jonathan Dickinson State Park, located off US 1 just south of the town of Hobe Sound.

End: Same place; this is a loop trail.

Camping: On the trail at the designated site. Campers must register with the ranger. Camping with all facilities is available at the state park.

Difficulty: Easy to moderate.

For Further Information: Jonathan Dickinson State Park, 16450 SE Federal Highway, Hobe Sound, FL 33455. (407) 546-2771

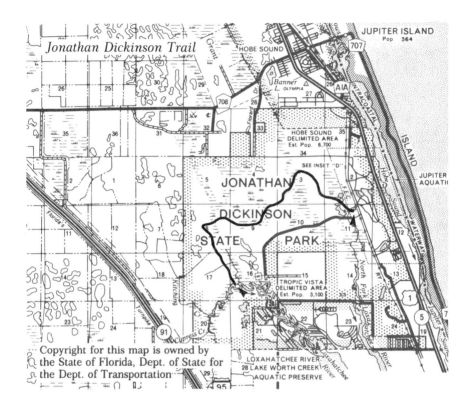

Marsh Nature Trail

Loxahatchee National Wildlife Refuge
Palm Beach County (near Delray Beach)
3.2 miles

The Marsh Nature Trail at the Loxahatchee National Wildlife Refuge provides a valuable introduction to the Everglades. *The Visitor's Guide*, an information booklet provided at the visitor's center, gives an excellent review of the characteristics of the cypress swamp and impounded marsh. The designated trail makes a circle around one of ten impoundments behind the visitor's center—a walk of less than one mile. Hikers can also walk around all ten impoundments if they wish, or encircle four of the interior impoundments, resulting in a trek of just over three miles. These areas are planted periodically with waterfowl food plants, and draining, burning, plowing, and reflooding also are part of the management plan. It is no wonder that many bird watchers rank this as one of the top five birding spots in Florida! The area is also rich in plant and animal life. Use *The Visitor's Guide* to identify birds, animals, and plants that you encounter.

This is a day-use-only area that is managed by the U.S. Fish and Wildlife Service.

Begin: At the Loxahatchee National Wildlife Refuge Visitor's Center, located ten miles west of the Florida Turnpike. It lies one mile west of US 441 between the points where SR 804 and SR 806 intersect that road.

End: Same place; this is a loop trail.

Camping: Not available.

Difficulty: Easy.

For Further Information: Loxahatchee National Wildlife Refuge, P.O. Box 2737, Delray Beach, FL 33437-2737.

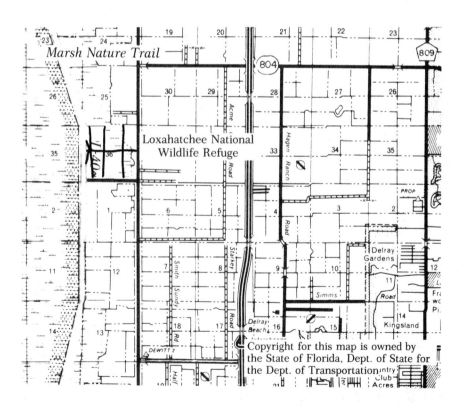

"Spite Highway"

Biscayne National Park
Dade County (near Miami)
North Route: 5 miles
South Route: 9 miles

Located seven miles offshore on Elliott Key, this trail's name hints at its interesting history. It was built by a group of island residents in 1968 in a vain attempt to develop the island and thus delay its purchase as part of Biscayne National Park. The only evidence of the "development" is this bulldozed swath cut through the center of the island, the planned site of a "highway" that would be built out of "spite."

There is no regularly scheduled transportation to and from the island so, once there, hikers often have the place to themselves: a wonderful opportunity to enjoy your own Atlantic island! Beginning at the Elliott Key Visitor's Center, hikers may walk 2.5 miles to the northern end of the island and return, or 4.5 miles to the southern end and return. Camping is permitted on the grounds of the visitor's center, where there are restrooms, cold-water showers, and potable water available. No open fires are permitted but fire rings are provided.

Transportation to the island may be arranged with the boating concessionaire at the Convoy Point Information Station at Biscayne National Park Headquarters.

Begin: At the Elliott Key Visitor's Center on Elliott Key, offshore from Biscayne National Park Headquarters, south of Miami.

End: Same place; the trail is a round-trip route.

Camping: Permitted at the visitor's center.

Difficulty: Easy.

For Further Information: Biscayne National Park, P.O. Box 1369, Homestead, FL 33090-1369.

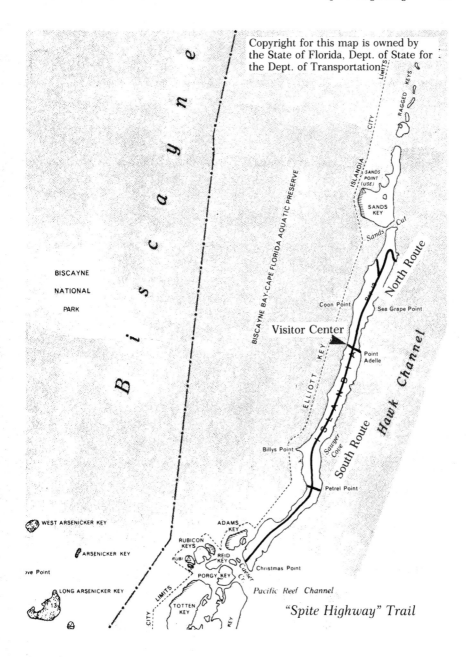

Copyright for this map is owned by
the State of Florida, Dept. of State for
the Dept. of Transportation

"Spite Highway" Trail

Trails of the Everglades

Everglades National Park
Dade, Monroe, Collier counties

The Miccosukee Indians called the everglades Pa-Hay-Okee, or "Grassy Waters." Marjory Stoneman Douglas named them the "River of Grass" and brought national attention to their plight in the 1940s. In 1947, over 2,200 square miles became Everglades National Park and in 1979, the United Nations declared the area a World Heritage Site. More than any other national park in America, Everglades must be seen from up close. It has a very special, very subtle beauty that requires a more intimate acquaintance than passing by in a car can provide. Walking or hiking is the best way to appreciate its variety and the park provides many opportunities to do so, from short walks to overnight trails.

As Mrs. Douglas informed us, the everglades are a huge, shallow, freshwater river some 50 miles wide and only a few inches deep. This river creeps slowly southward across the tip of Florida into Florida Bay and the Gulf of Mexico. Everglades National Park contains 1.4 million acres of many diverse natural environments. Besides the thousands of acres of open wet prairie covered with the long grasses of the glades, there are also forests of dwarf cypress growing on limestone ridges, slash pine plantations, and dense hardwood hammocks with immense mahogany trees and rare species of palms. The glades are also dotted with small ponds that are home to a vast population of birdlife. It is not unusual to see clouds of egrets, herons, and other waterbirds gathered around these holes. Other birds such as white and brown pelicans, roseate spoonbills, ospreys, and bald eagles may be seen near the saltwater inlets of Florida Bay. For those who know where to look, there is still an opportunity to see rare and unusual birds like Cape Sable sparrows, short-tailed hawks, peregrine falcons, and Florida mangrove cuckoos. Animals of the Everglades include those southern favorites: raccoons, opossums, skunks, armadillos, and an abundance of American alligators. The endangered Florida panther still ranges the area as well as a rare and highly threatened species of crocodile. Smaller animals of interest are the round-tail muskrats and many varieties of turtle.

The climate in the Everglades is subtropical. This enhances its unique position in North America as a home for plants and animals that are not seen elsewhere in the continental United States but it also creates problems for the unwary visitor. In the summer it is wet, humid, and very buggy; sudden afternoon thunderstorms are not at all unusual. The winter months are more pleasant with sunny mild days and cool evenings.

The longer trails in the Everglades National Park usually owe their existence to some earlier need for a "built-up" area across the glades such as an old access road to a community or the fill dirt that was pushed aside when a canal was built. Often these trails go through very wet areas and some wading may be required. Many of the shorter trails have been built specifically for the convenience of visitors to the park and may have boardwalks and other amenities to make the going easier. In either event, when walking these trails, it is essential to be prepared. Backcountry hiking requires registration with the ranger and it is wise to let someone else know where you plan to go, even for a few hours. The information centers provide maps, trail data, and up-to-the-minute information on weather and trail conditions. Check with them before setting out.

Trails in the Royal Palm Area

Slash Pine Trail: 7 miles
Loop Trail: 3 miles or 5 miles
Old Ingraham Highway: 11 miles

Both Slash Pine and Loop Trail are accessed from the road to Long Pine Key, which is only six miles from the main visitor's center outside of Homestead. They are appropriate for both hikers and bicyclists and follow a two-rut service road through an area of high pinelands. Over 200 varieties of plants grow under this pine canopy, 30 of which are said to be found nowhere else on earth.

The Old Ingraham Highway also begins on the Long Pine Key Road. It is the original road from Homestead to Flamingo and while it is no longer open to vehicular traffic, it is built up and usually dry. The trail begins in pinelands and traverses open glades as well as densely vegetated areas.

Begin/End: Slash Pine Trail begins at gate #4 on the Long Pine Key Road and continues for seven miles to the Main Park Road. *Loop Trail* begins at gate #3 on the Long Pine Key Road and travels for either three miles or five miles to locations on Hole-In-The-Doughnut Road near the Boy Scout Camp. *Old Ingraham Highway* is reached by driving 1.1 miles south on Long Pine Key Road. It ends on the Main Park Road 1.8 miles south of the turnoff to Mahogany Hammock.

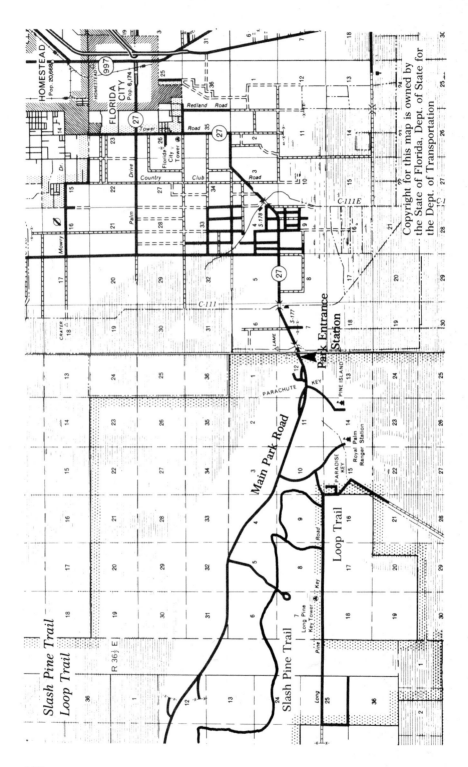

102

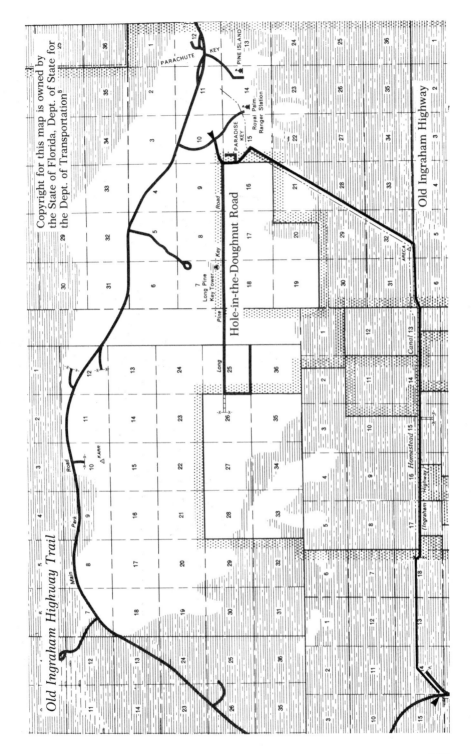

Old Ingraham Highway Trail

Hole-in-the-Doughnut Road

Old Ingraham Highway

PARACHUTE KEY

PINE ISLAND

PARADISE KEY

Royal Palm Ranger Station

Long Pine Key Tower

KARR

Park Road

Main Park Road

Pine Key Road

Long Key

Canal

Homestead

Ingraham Highway

ARECA

Camping: Camping is allowed on the trails with permission of the ranger.

Difficulty: Easy to moderate.

For Further Information: Visitor's Center, Everglades National Park, P.O. Box 279, Homestead, FL 33030.

Easy Walking Trails in the Flamingo Area

Snake Bight: 4 miles   *Bear Lake: 4 miles*
Rowdy Bend: 5 miles
Christian Point: 4 miles

All of these trail heads are in the Flamingo area, and are well marked. They traverse open prairies, mangrove swamps, and coastal flats to give a varied view of the many types of terrain in the southern section of the park. Snake Bight features a canopy of hardwoods and, at the end, a boardwalk that extends into Florida Bay. Rowdy Bend has coastal prairies and palm trees as well as ghostly Spanish moss draped over the limbs of hardwoods. The Christian Point Trail has a dense stretch of mangroves, giant wild pine bromeliads clinging to trees, and open coastal prairies. The Bear Lake Trail is a result of an effort to drain land and was made from fill dirt from the Homestead Canal.

Begin: *Snake Bight* Trail begins about six miles northeast of the Flamingo Ranger Station on the Main Park Road. *Rowdy Bend Trail* begins about three miles northeast of the Flamingo Ranger Station on the Main Park Road. *Christian Point Trail* begins about one and one half miles northeast of the Flamingo Ranger Station off the Main Park Road. All have signs and parking areas for vehicles.

Bear Lake Trail begins about three miles north of the Flamingo Ranger Station off Bear Lake Road. To reach it, turn left onto Bear Lake Road at its intersection with the Main Park Road and travel for almost two miles to the end of the road. The trail is on the west side and is marked.

End: All of these trails return to their points of origin, but it is possible to make a loop of Rowdy Bend and Snake Bight since they connect with each other.

Camping: Not permitted on the trails. Camping is available at nearby Flamingo Campground.

Difficulty: Easy.

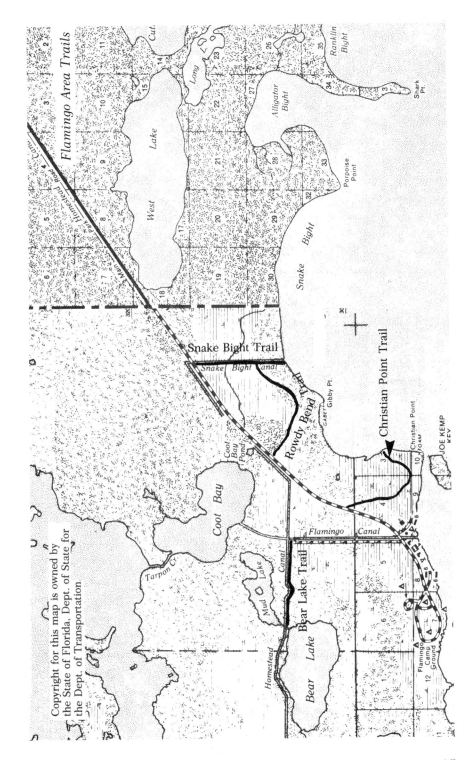

Flamingo Area Trails

Snake Bight Trail

Christian Point Trail

Rowdy Bend Trail

Bear Lake Trail

Snake Bight Canal

West Lake

Long Lake

Cut.

Ranklin Bight

Shark Pt.

Alligator Bight

Porpoise Point

Snake Bight

Gibby Pt.

Christian Point

JOE KEMP KEY

Coot Bay Pond

Coot Bay

Tarpon C.

Mud Lake

Homestead Canal

Bear Lake

Flamingo Canal

Flamingo Camp Ground

Longer Hikes in the Flamingo Area

Coastal Prairie Trail: 12 miles
Alligator Creek Trail: 14.6 miles

The Coastal Prairie Trail is also in the Flamingo area but is longer and more difficult than those mentioned above. It follows the path of a road that once went to Cape Sable and traverses miles of open salt marsh and buttonwood forest. Although the trail bed is built up, some sections frequently are wet. The trail ends at Clubhouse Beach where the foundation of a clubhouse erected in 1912 still stands. Camping is permitted there, but potable water and other facilities are not available.

Begin: At Flamingo Campground.

End: Same place; this is a round-trip route.

Camping: Permitted at Clubhouse Beach.

Difficulty: Moderate to strenuous.

The *Alligator Creek Trail,* in the same section, is an excellent backcountry trail. It was built in the 1930s to allow cotton pickers access to the area to remove the wild cotton plants. These plants, which are still a problem in agriculture, have infestations of pine boll worms, which can spread to commercial cotton fields.

The trail follows the Snake Bight Canal, then passes through coastal prairie and hardwood forests to Alligator Creek. This is a primitive camping area that is also accessible from the West Lake Canoe Trail. A permit is required for camping.

Begin: At Snake Bight Canal Road.

End: Same place; this is a round-trip route.

Camping: At Alligator Creek campsite. No potable water or facilities. Register with the ranger.

Difficulty: Moderate to strenuous.

For Further Information: Visitor's Center, Everglades National Park, P.O. Box 279, Homestead, FL 33030.

Trails in the Shark Valley Area

Tram Road: 15 miles

The Shark Valley is primarily a shallow waterway that is the headwaters for the Shark River. As a result, it is wet and generally inappropriate for hiking. The Tram Road has been built up for public usage, however, and is available for hiking and bicycling as well as for a roadway for the tram ride.

Begin/End: Hikers usually choose to walk counterclockwise so that they meet the tram tour rather than have it approach from behind them. Both ends of the road begin at the Shark Valley Information Center.

Camping: Not permitted on the Tram Road.

Difficulty: Easy to moderate.

For Further Information: Visitor's Center, Everglades National Park, P.O. Box 279, Homestead, FL 33030.

Butch Horn

Trail head at Rowdy Bend Trail, Everglades National Park

Big Cypress Trail, South

Big Cypress National Preserve
Collier County (near Naples)
27 miles

Big Cypress Preserve is a vast continuation of the Everglades that
provides unique recreational opportunities to the hiker: the chal-
lenge of extremely remote territory. Its terrain ranges from grassy
prairie to dense forest stands. Big Cypress allows experienced hikers
truly to get away from it all. The preserve encompasses almost 600,000
acres of wilderness and is the last habitat for a number of endangered
species, including the famous Florida panther. The Big Cypress Trail
was built and is maintained by the Florida Trail Association and is blazed
with the FTA's characteristic orange blazes. The return trail is blazed in
blue.

While the trail is within the boundaries of the preserve, there are
still some outholdings of private property that it crosses. These
outholdings are relics of the Florida "Land Boom" of the early part of the
century, when swampland was commonly subdivided and sold to buyers
who were far away. Most of these "lots" have no access and it would be
almost impossible for their owners to identify them without a surveyor in
tow. As a result, they are included as a part of the Big Cypress Trail,
South. The same situation is not true for the northern part of the trail. In
that area, private ownership is a problem and access to many parts of the
trail is open only to FTA members. Non-members should not continue
beyond the blue-blazed trail.

Hikers planning to use the Big Cypress, South Trail should have a
compass and map and should register with the ranger at the Oasis
Ranger Station. Camping is permitted on the trail and water is available
from pumps at miles 7 and 17.

Begin: At the Oasis Ranger Station on US 41 east of Naples.

End: Same place; this is a loop trail.

Camping: Permitted on the trail. Register with the ranger.

Difficulty: Moderate to strenuous.

For Further Information: Big Cypress National Preserve, HCR 61,
Box 10, Ochopee, FL 33943. (813) 262-1066

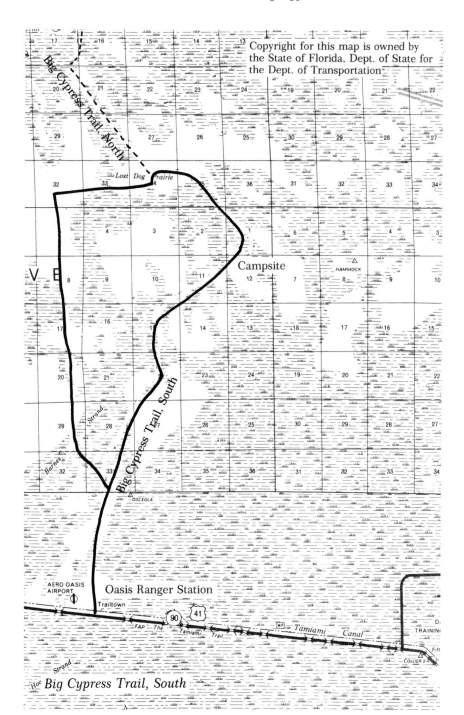

Big Cypress Trail, South

Fakahatchee Strand Trail

Fakahatchee Strand State Preserve
Collier County (near Naples)
10 miles

The Fakahatchee Strand is a continuation of Big Cypress Swamp that is being purchased by the state of Florida. The Strand is about 20 miles long and is 3 to 5 miles wide. When the acquisition is complete, it will stretch from Alligator Alley to the north, to Everglades National Park to the south. It contains the largest stand of royal palms and the largest concentration and variety of orchids in North America. Many other species of rare plants grow in the preserve, and the Florida panther makes its home there as well. The Strand is very wet and very wild. Nature tours called "swamp walks" or "guided wades" are led by a ranger on Tuesdays through Saturdays, with two weeks advance reservation required.

The trail follows the bed of an old logging railroad and is almost a straight line for ten miles. For the first few miles it shows evidence of off-road vehicles, but it soon becomes overgrown and difficult to follow. It may be wet in places and spur lines that lead away from the main trail can be misleading. A compass and map are essential. It is best to take the "swamp walk" or "guided wade" with the ranger before setting out on your own—an excellent way to become acquainted with the terrain.

Begin: Three miles west of the intersection of Alligator Alley (SR 84) and SR 29.

End: On W. J. Janes Memorial Scenic Drive off SR 29 near Copeland.

Camping: Permitted, but there are no facilities or potable water.

Difficulty: Moderate to strenuous.

For Further Information: Fakahatchee Strand State Preserve, P.O. Box 548, Copeland, FL 33926. (813) 695-4593

Fakahatchee Strand Trail

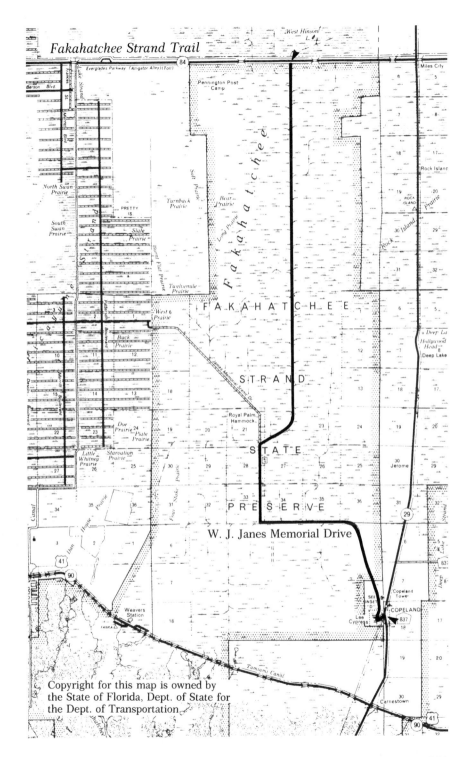

W. J. Janes Memorial Drive

Collier-Seminole Trail

Collier-Seminole State Park
Collier County (near Naples)
6.6 miles

Collier-Seminole is on the western edge of the Everglades and is an almost impenetrable wilderness of mangrove swamp, cypress swamp, and freshwater marsh. The Florida Trail Association has blazed and assists in the maintenance of the 6.6 miles of trail that were built on areas of higher ground. Even so, it is frequently wet, and as on all Everglades trails, the insects can be vicious. The 4,800 acres of protected wilderness provide a home for Florida black bear, mangrove fox squirrel, and the Florida panther. The stately royal palm tree grows naturally here as well.

The trail is a loop beginning at a locked gate south of the park entrance on US 41. Hikers must register with the ranger before setting out. The main trail is blazed in white, while the return trails are blazed in blue. There is a designated campsite with an established campfire ring. Fires in other locations are not permitted. Food must be suspended from trees to discourage bears and there is no potable water available on the trail.

Begin: At Collier-Seminole State Park, 17 miles south of Naples on US 41. Trail head is beyond locked gate on your left, about three-quarters of a mile south of park entrance.

End: Same place; this is a loop trail.

Camping: At the designated campsite on the trail, or at the state park.

Difficulty: Moderate to strenuous.

For Further Information: Collier-Seminole State Park, 19800 E. Tamiami Trail, Naples, FL 33961. (813) 394-3397

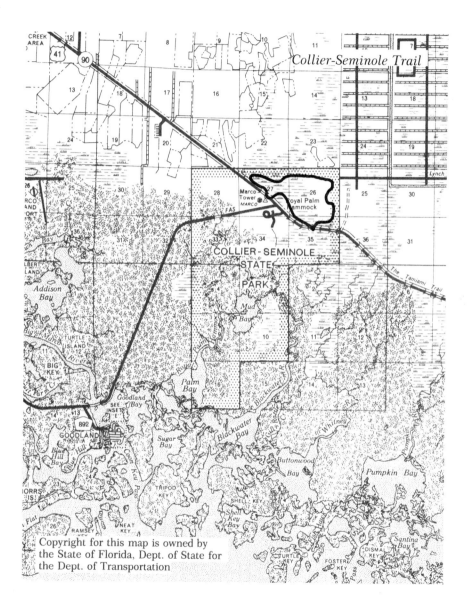

Myakka Trail

Myakka River State Park
Sarasota, Manatee counties (near Sarasota)
38 miles

Myakka River is the largest state park in Florida, consisting of almost 30,000 acres. It is a beautiful area with a large, shallow lake and the rambling Myakka River to provide aquatic interest. The trail is relatively flat and may be wet during the rainy season. It passes through pine flatwoods, dry prairies, oak-palm hammocks and marsh land. It is not unusual to see deer and turkey along the way, as well as a great variety of birds. The endangered bald eagle and sandhill crane use habitat in the area.

The trail was built in cooperation with the Florida Trail Association and is marked with blue and white blazes. It consists of four loops: Bee Island, Honore, Deer Prairie, and East Loop. The Bee Island loop is 11.2 miles long—a nice hike for those who do not have the time or inclination to walk the entire 38 miles. There are four designated campsites: Bee Island, Honore, Panther Point, and Oak Grove. All have pitcher-pump-equipped wells nearby, but this water should be purified for drinking. Only 12 campers are permitted at each campsite and all hikers should register with the ranger before setting out. A small camping fee is charged.

Begin: At Myakka River State Park, 17 miles east of Sarasota off SR 72.

End: Same place; this is a loop trail.

Camping: There are four designated campsites with unpurified well water on the trail. Camping with all facilities is available at the State Park.

Difficulty: Easy to moderate.

For Further Information: Myakka River State Park, 13207 S.R. 72, Sarasota, FL 34241. (813) 361-6511

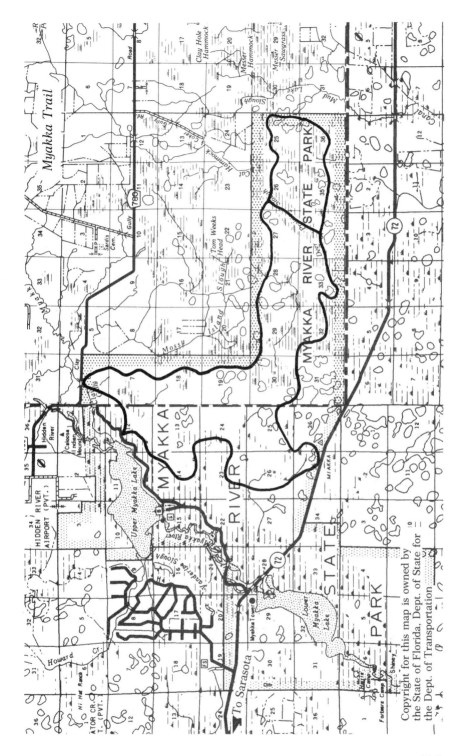

Sanibel-Captiva Trail

Sanibel-Captiva Conservation Center
Lee County (near Ft. Myers)
4.15 miles

The Sanibel-Captiva Conservation Foundation is a nonprofit organization that maintains a beautiful visitor's center, native plant nursery, and nature trail on Sanibel Island. In this highly developed area of the state, this 200-acre oasis provides an opportunity to see an ancient "beach ridge" community. The trail is especially designed to acquaint visitors with the many varieties of plants that are encountered in this type of environment. There also is an observation tower, which makes a fine vantage point for bird watching. Although this is a privately owned facility, it is open to the public.

The Sanibel-Captiva Trail is actually ten short trails that interconnect, allowing the hiker to walk from 0.26 miles on the Middle Ridge Trail, to the full 4.15 miles when all ten trails are combined. The visitor's center has an excellent self-guiding booklet, *Walk in the Wetlands*, which is very useful for identifying plants seen along the trails.

Begin: At the Sanibel-Captiva Conservation Center, off Sanibel-Captiva Road. Sanibel Island is offshore from Ft. Myers.

End: Same place; these are loop trails.

Camping: Not available.

Difficulty: Easy.

For Further Information: The Sanibel-Captiva Conservation Foundation, P.O. Box 839, Sanibel, FL 33957. (813) 472-2329

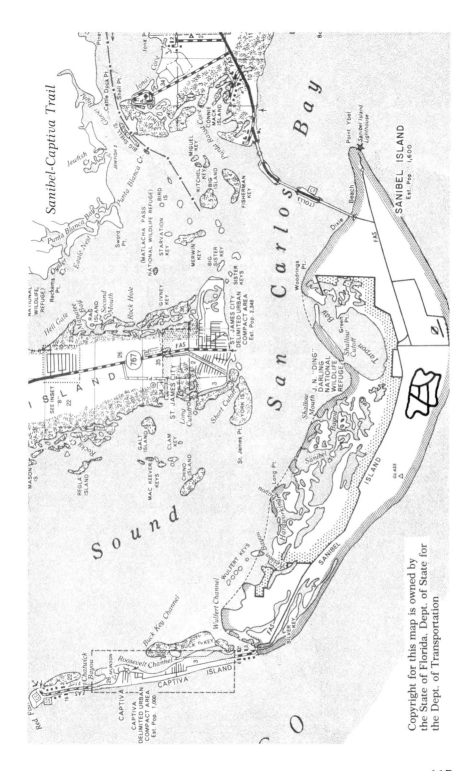

Sanibel-Captiva Trail

Other Trails

Other Trails

In addition to the trails annotated in this directory, there were several others that deserve mention and further investigation:

Corkscrew Swamp Sanctuary is a wilderness area owned and maintained by the National Audubon Society. It is located 14 miles from Immokalee and is open to the public from 9 AM to 5 PM daily. There is a fee for admission. It features a boardwalk loop almost two miles long through a bald cypress stand. For information, contact the Chief Naturalist, Corkscrew Swamp Sanctuary, Rt. 6, Box 1875-A, Naples, FL 33999.

Felix Lake Nature Trail is located on the Tyndall Air Force Base near Panama City and is a designated National Recreation Trail. It is marked and is two to three miles long. It encircles a freshwater lake that is said to contain numerous alligators. For more information, contact Joe Taylor at the Bonita Bay Recreation Area, (904)283-4359; or write to Morale, Welfare and Recreation, Department of the Air Force, Tyndall Air Force Base, FL 32403-5000.

Fort Pierce Inlet Recreation Area has an interesting trail built on walkways that lead through mangroves and marsh to Jack Island. It is just under three miles long. Ft. Pierce Inlet State Recreation Area is four miles east of Ft. Pierce off SR A1A.

Ravine State Gardens are located in the town of Palatka. This is part of a very beautiful and unusual geologic phenomenon that has been enhanced by the planting of thousands of plants by the Federal Works Project Administration in 1933. The auto road around the upper rim is a two-mile loop, while the trail into the ravine is one mile long. Ravine State Gardens, P.O. Box 1096, Palatka, FL 32077.

Larry and Penny Thompson Memorial Park is located in metropolitan Miami and is owned and administered by the Metro-Dade Park and Recreation Department. It has a five-mile bike-and-hiking trail that bypasses a lake and includes a physical fitness loop. This is a highly urban area and a well-used facility, but it does provide city-dwellers an opportunity to take a hike in an area not bothered by vehicle traffic.

Turkey Lake Park is located in the city of Orlando and has seven miles of nature trails that meander through live oak hammocks and cattail marshes. Again, it is in an urban area and is well used; but it is a pleasant place for an outing.

University Nature Trails are located on the campus of the University of North Florida at Jacksonville and are designated as a National Recreational Trail. There are four trails that provide an opportunity for a hike of up to 12 miles. The university campus is a wildlife refuge and contributes to the outdoor recreation environment by providing these trails in this urban setting. For further information, contact the University of North Florida, P.O. Box 17074, Jacksonville, FL 32318.

St. Marks Rail Trail is a project currently under construction under the auspices of the national Rails to Trails Conservancy and the Florida Department of Natural Resources. Located on the site of the abandoned St. Marks railroad bed, it will be 16 miles long, stretching from the southern edge of the city of Tallahassee to the village of St. Marks. It will be suitable for hiking, biking, and horseback riding. For further information, contact the Department of Natural Resources, Marjory Stoneman Douglas Building, Commonwealth Boulevard, Tallahassee, FL 32301.

Bibliography

Bell, C. R. and B. J. Taylor. *Florida Wildflowers and Roadside Plants.* Chapel Hill, N.C.: Laurel Hill Press, 1982.

Carter, E. F. and J. L. Pearce. *A Canoeing and Kayaking Guide to the Streams of Florida*, vol. 1. Birmingham: Menasha Ridge Press, 1985.

DeLorme Publications. *Florida Atlas and Gazeteer.* Freeport, Maine: 1986.

Fernald, E. A., ed. *Atlas of Florida.* Tallahassee: Rose Printing Company, 1981.

Florida Board of Forestry. *Trees of Florida.* Tallahassee, 1981.

Florida State Road Department. *Early Highways of Florida.* Tallahassee, 1951.

Grow, Gerald. *Florida Parks.* Tallahassee: Longleaf Publications, 1981.

Keller, J. M. *Walking the Florida Trail*, rev. ed. Gainesville: Florida Trail Association, 1985.

Lane, J. A. *A Birder's Guide to Florida.* Denver: L and P Press, 1984.

Martin, R. L. *Motorist's Guide to Everglades National Park.* Homestead, Fla.: Everglades Natural History Association, 1983.

Morris, A. *Florida Handbook: 1985–86.* Tallahassee: Peninsular Publishing Company, 1986.

Peutz, C. J. *Florida County Maps and Recreational Guide.* Lyndon Station, Wis.: C. J. Peutz.

Rosenau, J. C., G. L. Faulkner, C. W. Hendry, Jr., and R. W. Hull. *Springs of Florida.* Tallahassee: U.S. Geological Survey, Bureau of Geology, Florida Department of Natural Resources, 1978.

Tarver, D. P., J. A. Rodgers, M. M. Mahler, and R. L. Lazor. *Aquatic and Wetland Plants of Florida.* Tallahassee: Florida Department of Natural Resources, 1979.

Watts, B. M. *Watery Wilderness of Apalach, Florida.* Tallahassee: Apalach Books, 1975.

Williams, W. *Florida's Fabulous Waterbirds.* Tampa: World-Wide Publishing, 1983.

Index of Trails

About the Author

Elizabeth F. Carter is a native Floridian who has been enjoying the outdoors all of her life. She is the co-author of *A Canoeing and Kayaking Guide to the Streams of Florida, Vol. I,* and the author of *Downriver Canoeing in Florida's Big Bend* as well as numerous articles on canoeing, hiking, and camping for outdoors magazines. She is a founding member and former president of the Apalachee Canoe Club and an officer in the Florida Canoeing and Kayaking Association. She is also president of Downriver Canoeing, Inc., an outdoor guide service in Tallahassee.